# MAP READING AND LOCAL STUDIES

## IN COLOUR

No.24.

**A. P. FULLAGAR** B.A.

*Head of Geography Department,*
*The John Cleveland College,*
*Hinckley, Leicestershire*

**H. E. VIRGO** M.A.

*Vice Principal,*
*The John Cleveland College,*
*Hinckley, Leicestershire*

ISBN 0 340 18665 8
First edition 1967
Second edition 1975

Printed in Great Britain for
Hodder and Stoughton Educational,
a division of Hodder and Stoughton Ltd,
Mill Road, Dunton Green, Sevenoaks, Kent TN13 2YD,
by W. S. Cowell Ltd, Ipswich

**HODDER AND STOUGHTON**
LONDON   SYDNEY   AUCKLAND   TORONTO

# ORDNANCE SURVEY SYMBOL CHARTS

## Key for 1:50 000 maps

### ROADS AND PATHS

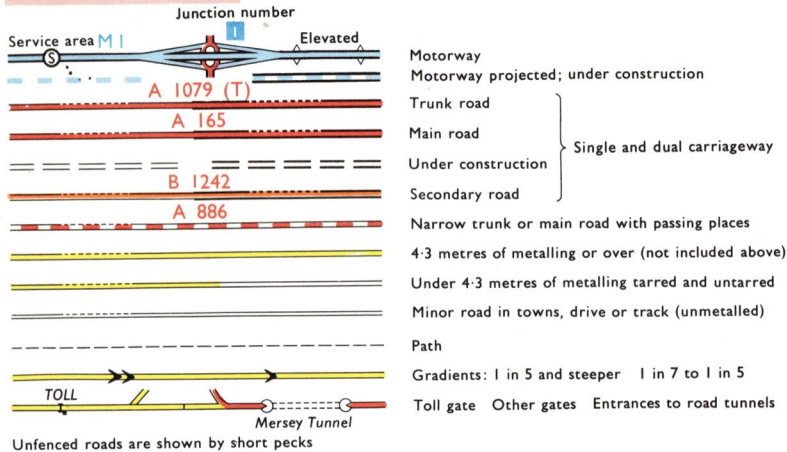

Motorway
Motorway projected; under construction
Trunk road
Main road
Under construction
Secondary road
}
Single and dual carriageway

Narrow trunk or main road with passing places
4·3 metres of metalling or over (not included above)
Under 4·3 metres of metalling tarred and untarred
Minor road in towns, drive or track (unmetalled)
Path
Gradients: 1 in 5 and steeper    1 in 7 to 1 in 5
Toll gate    Other gates    Entrances to road tunnels

Unfenced roads are shown by short pecks

### PUBLIC RIGHTS OF WAY

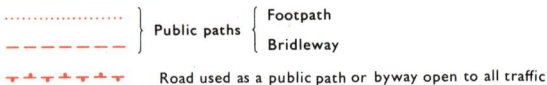
Public paths { Footpath / Bridleway

Road used as a public path or byway open to all traffic

Public rights of way indicated by these symbols have been derived from Definitive Maps as amended by later enactments or instruments held by Ordnance Survey on   1st July 1972   , and are shown subject to the limitations imposed by the scale of mapping

The representation on this map of any other road, track or path is no evidence of the existence of a right of way

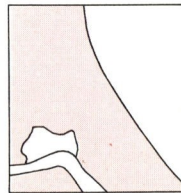
Extent of available information.

### RAILWAYS

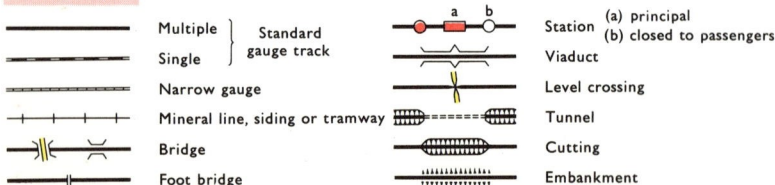

| | |
|---|---|
| Multiple | Standard gauge track |
| Single | |
| Narrow gauge | |
| Mineral line, siding or tramway | |
| Bridge | |
| Foot bridge | |

Station (a) principal (b) closed to passengers
Viaduct
Level crossing
Tunnel
Cutting
Embankment

### WATER FEATURES

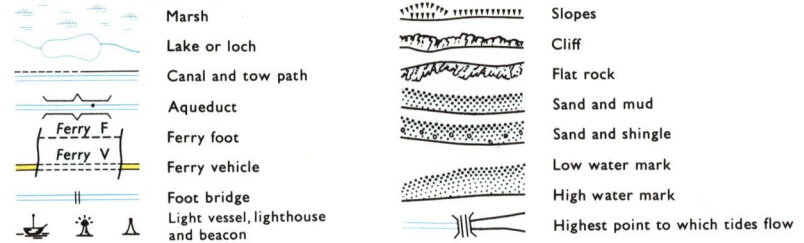

Marsh
Lake or loch
Canal and tow path
Aqueduct
Ferry foot
Ferry vehicle
Foot bridge
Light vessel, lighthouse and beacon

Slopes
Cliff
Flat rock
Sand and mud
Sand and shingle
Low water mark
High water mark
Highest point to which tides flow

### GENERAL FEATURES

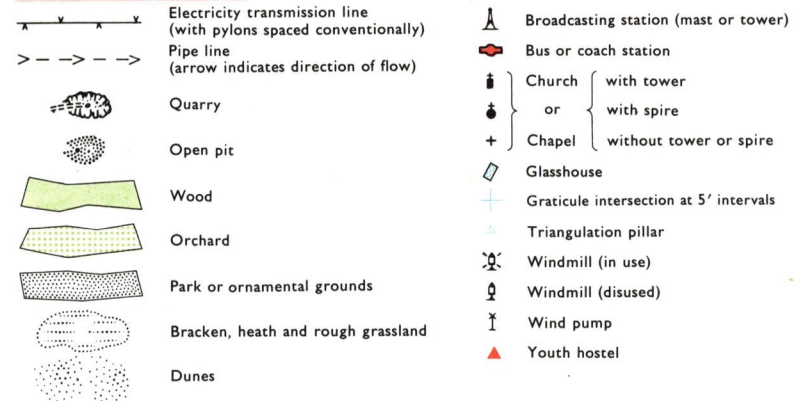

Electricity transmission line (with pylons spaced conventionally)
Pipe line (arrow indicates direction of flow)
Quarry
Open pit
Wood
Orchard
Park or ornamental grounds
Bracken, heath and rough grassland
Dunes

Broadcasting station (mast or tower)
Bus or coach station
Church { with tower } or { with spire } Chapel { without tower or spire
Glasshouse
Graticule intersection at 5′ intervals
Triangulation pillar
Windmill (in use)
Windmill (disused)
Wind pump
Youth hostel

### RELIEF

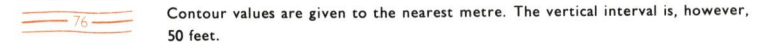

Contour values are given to the nearest metre. The vertical interval is, however, 50 feet.

.144    Heights are to the nearest metre above mean sea level. Heights shown close to a triangulation pillar refer to the station height at ground level and not necessarily to the summit. Details of the summit height may be obtained from the Ordnance Survey
1 metre = 3·2808 feet          15·24 metres = 50 feet

### BOUNDARIES

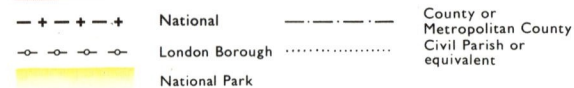

National
London Borough
National Park
County or Metropolitan County
Civil Parish or equivalent

The county areas and names shown on this map are effective on 1st April 1974
Urban Civil Parishes cease to exist on 1st April 1974

National Trust { always open / opening restricted }

2

## ABBREVIATIONS

| | | | |
|---|---|---|---|
| P | Post office | TH | Town hall, Guildhall or equivalent |
| PH | Public house | PC | Public convenience (in rural areas) |
| CH | Club house | .T | Telephone call box PO |
| .MP | Mile post | .A | Telephone call box AA |
| .MS | Mile stone | .R | Telephone call box RAC |

## ANTIQUITIES

| | | | |
|---|---|---|---|
| VILLA | Roman | + | Site of antiquity |
| Cumulus | Non-Roman | ⚔ 1066 | Battlefield (with date) |

## SCALE

**1:50 000**

2 centimetres to 1 kilometre (one grid square)

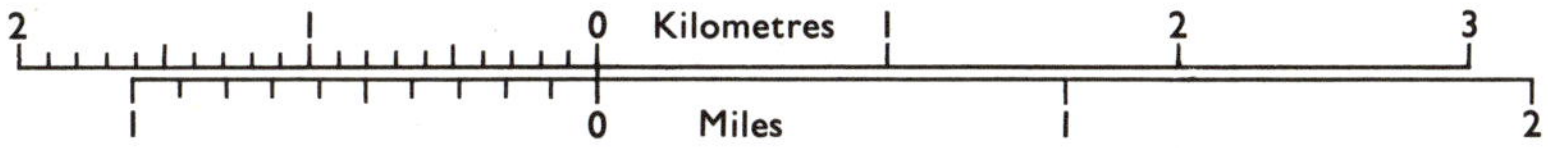

2
1
0
Kilometres
1
2
3
1
0
Miles
1
2


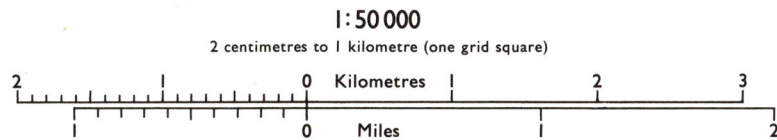

1 kilometre = 0·6214 mile

1 mile = 1·6093 kilometres



## Key for 1:25 000 maps

### *Roads*

| | | |
|---|---|---|
| *Motorway, Trunk and Main Road (Dual Carriageway)* | M4 or A6(M) | A123 or A123(T) |
| *Trunk & Main Road* | A123 or A123(T) | |
| *Secondary Road* | *Fenced* B2314 | *Unfenced* |
| *Road Under Construction* | | |
| *Other Roads* | *Good, metalled* | *Poor, or unmetalled* |
| *Footpaths* | *FP Fenced* | *FP Unfenced* |

*Railways, Multiple Track*

" *Single Track*

" *Narrow Gauge*

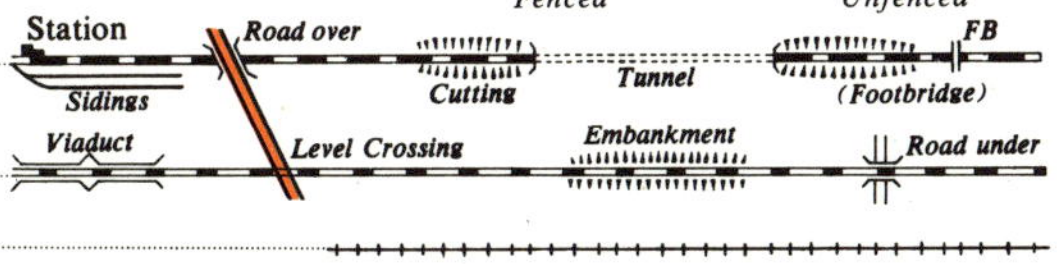

Station
Sidings
Road over
Cutting
Tunnel
FB
(Footbridge)
Viaduct
Level Crossing
Embankment
Road under


*London & Glasgow Transport Underground Stations* ....... *Interchange Stations* .......

*Aerial Ropeway* ....... *Aerial Ropeway*

*Boundaries* { *County or County Borough* — — — — —
" " *County of City (in Scotland)*

" " " " " " *with Parish* —·—·—·—

" *Parish* · · · · · · · ·

*Pipe Line (Oil, Water)* ....... *Pipe Line*

*Electricity Transmission Lines (Pylons shown at bends and spaced conventionally)* —⊠— — — — —⊠—

*Post Offices (In Villages & Rural Areas only)* ....... P *Town Hall* ....... TH *Public House* ....... PH

*Church or Chapel with Tower* ....... *Church or Chapel with Spire* ....... *Church or Chapel without either* ....... ✚

*Triangulation Station* ....... △ *on Church with Tower* ....... *without Tower* .......

*Intersected Point on Chy* ....... ⊙ *on Church with Spire* ....... *without Spire* ....... ✚ *on Building* .......

*Guide Post* ....... GP. *Mile Post* ....... MP. *Mile Stone* ....... MS. *Boundary Stone* ....... BS ∘ *Boundary Post* ....... BP∘

*Youth Hostel* ....... Y *Telephone Call Box (Public)* ....... T *(AA)* ....... A *(RAC)* ....... R *Antiquity (site of)* .......

*Public Buildings* .......

*Quarry & Gravel Pit* .......

*National Trust Area* ....... Sheen Common NT

" " " *Scotland* ....... NTS

*Osier Bed* .......

*Reeds* .......

*Park, Fenced* .......

*Wood, Coniferous, Fenced* .......

*Wood, Non-Coniferous Unfenced* .......

*Brushwood, Fenced & Unfenced* .......

*Glasshouses* .......

*Orchard* .......

*Furze* .......

*Rough Pasture Heath & Moor* .......

*Marsh* .......

*Well* ....... W ∘

*Spring* ....... Spr ∘

*Wind Pump* ....... Wd Pp.

*Contours are at 25 feet vertical interval.*

*Spot Height* ....... 123·

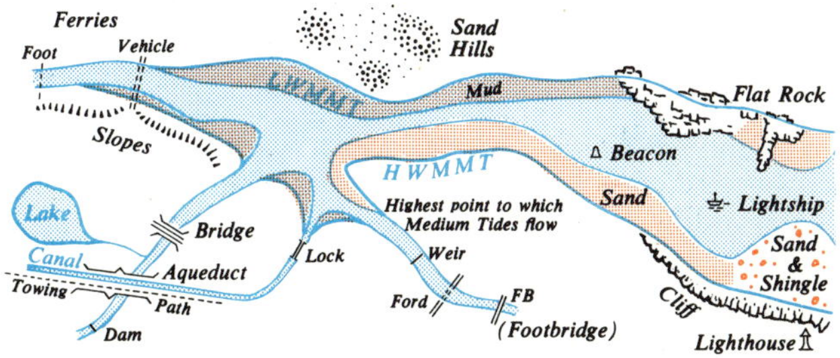

Ferries
Foot
Vehicle
Sand Hills
Mud
LWMMT
Flat Rock
Slopes
HWMMT
Beacon
Lake
Sand
Lightship
Highest point to which Medium Tides flow
Bridge
Canal
Lock
Weir
Sand & Shingle
Aqueduct
Towing Path
Ford
FB
Cliff
Dam
(Footbridge)
Lighthouse


*(High & Low Water Mark of Ordinary Spring Tides, in Scotland)*

# THE MECHANICS OF MAP READING

**National Grid:** Ordnance Survey maps are covered by a grid or pattern of parallel lines, one kilometre apart. The lines running from north to south are known as eastings and those from east to west as northings. Points on the map can be located by grid references as shown in figure 1. Four-figure references are used to identify grid squares. The first two figures are an easting (vertical line) and the last two a northing (horizontal line). The easting and northing form an L around the square. Six-figure references are used to locate exact points on a map. The first three figures represent the easting and the last three the northing, the third and sixth figures being the number of tenths.

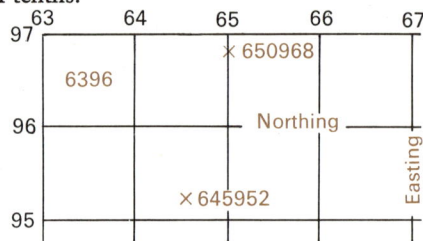

**FIGURE I**
**Four and six figure references**

**Scale:** The scale of a map is the relationship between the distance on the map and the equivalent distance on the ground. For example, on a map which has a representative fraction of 1:50 000, one centimetre on the map is equivalent to 50 000 centimetres (or ½ kilometre) on the ground.

**Measurement of Distance:** To measure the length of winding roads or rivers, take a straight edge of paper and mark the starting point towards the left end with a sharp pencil; then twist the edge along the course you are measuring, using the pencil at intervals as a pivot.

**Direction and Bearings:** Direction can be expressed (a) by means of compass points, or (b) in degrees as a three-figure bearing measured from north in a clockwise direction. Remember that a compass shows magnetic north, which in Britain is west of true north. The direction of the north–south grid lines is approximately true north, the slight difference being given at the bottom of each Ordnance Survey map.

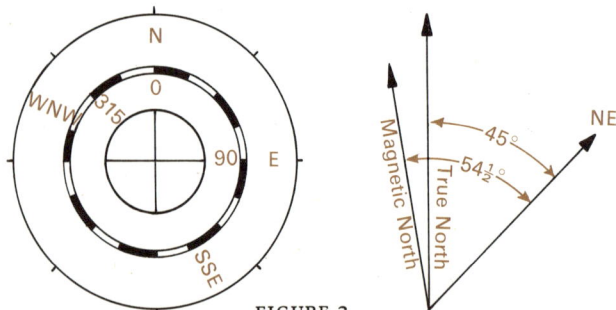

**FIGURE 2**
**Compass points and bearings**

*Exercise :* Study figure 2 which is incomplete. Make a copy of this diagram and then add all the compass points and bearings which are marked off.

**Setting a Map:** To set a map in the field with a compass, place the compass on the map when spread out flat. Then turn the map until the compass needle is lined up with magnetic north marked on the margin of the map. The map is then set. Without a compass, the map can be set if you can locate your own position and a prominent feature both on the map and in the field. A distant church is ideal for this purpose. Turn the map until a line from your position on the map through the identified feature is pointing to the actual feature in the field.

**Contours and Land Forms**
Relief is the shape of the land's surface, and the contour pattern is the main means of interpreting it on a map. Contours are lines joining places of equal height above sea level. The contour interval is the difference in height between adjacent contours. The density of contours indicates the degree of slope. When contours are close together the slope is steep, and when they are far apart the slope is gentle. Concave slopes are steep at the higher part becoming less steep lower down while convex slopes are gentler higher up becoming steeper lower down. Stepped slopes are those which have a succession of gentle stretches followed by steeper ones. Precipitous slopes are extremely steep, so much so that contour lines may converge and map makers may abandon them in favour of a symbol.

**Cross Sections:** These are scale drawings representing the view as it would appear from the side if a cut had been made through the land surface along a given line. In order to show the relief features clearly, the vertical scale is exaggerated in relation to the horizontal scale. Thus the vertical scale may be 1cm for 100m and the horizontal scale 1cm for 1km. In this case the exaggeration is 1km divided by 100m, which is 10 times.

An accurate cross section involves plotting every contour height along the line of the section, as shown in figure 3. Such a cross section is often used to determine whether one point on a map is visible from another. A sketch section, on the other hand, can be drawn 'by eye', either with a very limited number of fixed points or no measurements at all.

**How to draw a Cross Section:** Place the edge of a piece of paper along the line of the section on the map. Mark on the paper where the contours cut its edge and number every mark with its height. Then place the paper along the base of a prepared lined paper similar to that illustrated in figure 3. Then erect perpendiculars to the appropriate height and join these up.

**Gradient:** This is the degree of slope. We estimate it by first measuring the distance over which the gradient is required. It may be along a road, in which case remember to measure along the course of the road and not in a straight line. Then work out the difference in height between the two ends using the evidence of the contours and spot heights. If one point is halfway between a 259- and a 274-metre contour, assume the height to be 266½ metres. In the case of a distance of 2km 300m, with a difference in height of 326m, first bring the distance to metres. The gradient is then 326 divided by 2300 or approximately 1 in 7.

**Contour Patterns:** When endeavouring to visualise the relief of an area from evidence on the map, use all the information available. This includes not only con-

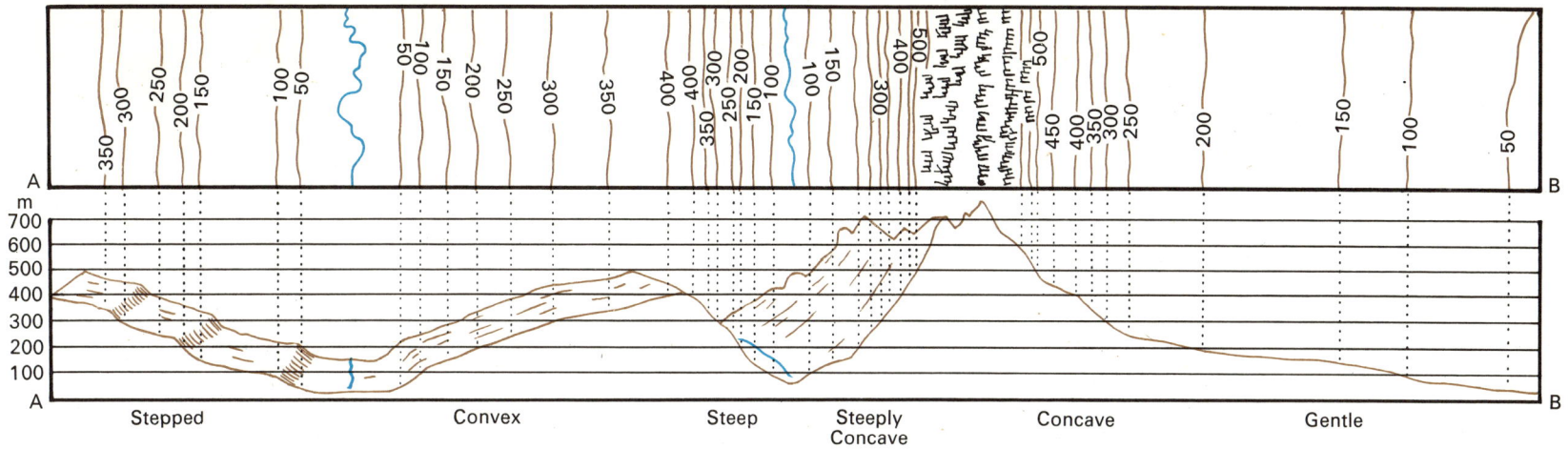

FIGURE 3

**Slopes and sections**

tour heights, spot heights and trigonometrical points, but also the drainage and contour patterns. Remember for example that contours are likely to point up towards high land when they bend around a river course.

*Exercise*: Each of the following definitions of land forms is illustrated in figure 4. Redraw this diagram accurately using the help of the grid lines and then label each feature in the correct place. The contour interval is 50 metres; mark the heights against the contours which have not been numbered.

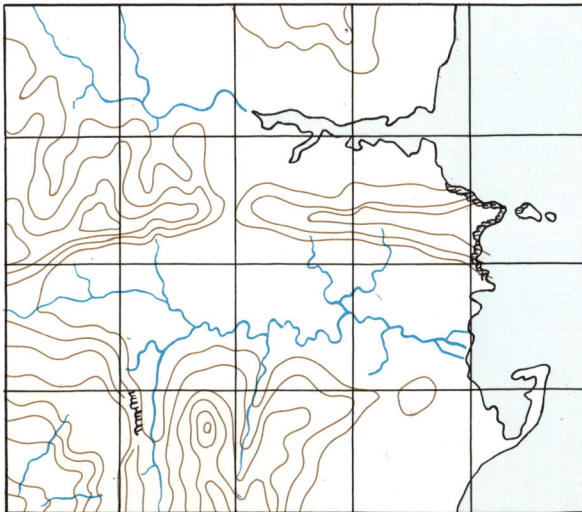

FIGURE 4

**Some definitions of land forms:**

*Ridge*. A long, narrow area of high land.

*Convex slope*. A slope that is steep at the bottom, becoming less steep higher up.

*Concave slope*. A slope that is steep at the top, becoming less steep lower down.

*Promontory*. High land jutting out to sea and sometimes known as a headland.

*Cliff*. A precipitous slope.

*Estuary*. A wide river mouth.

*Bay*. A large coastal inlet.

*Cove*. A small coastal inlet.

*Col* or *Saddle*. A dip between two summits; a high pass through a range of hills or mountains.

*Gap* or *Pass*. A low way through high land.

*Peak*. The highest point of a steep-sided hill.

*Valley*. A narrow depression with a sloping bottom, open at the lower end, and normally occupied by a river.

*Gorge*. A narrow, deep valley with very steep sides, sometimes nearly vertical.

*Delta*. An area of alluvium at the mouth of a river crossed by a number of channels or distributaries of that river.

*Fleet* or *Lagoon*. A shallow stretch of water partly or completely separated from the sea by a narrow strip of land.

*Confluence*. The joining of two watercourses.

*Meander*. The pronounced winding of a river.

*Plateau*. A flat area of high land.

*Knoll*. A low, detached hill.

*Cuesta*. A ridge with a steep slope on one side (known as the scarp slope) and a gentle slope on the other side (the dip slope).

*Spur*. A long, narrow projection of high land into low land.

*Stack*. A small, rocky island near to the coastline and separated from it as a result of marine erosion.

# ROCKS AND DRAINAGE

**The character of rocks:** It is generally impossible to determine the actual type of rock in any given area from evidence given on an Ordnance Survey map. We can only make informed suggestions as to what types of rock might be represented. However, with experience it is possible to look for clues which help to identify a probable rock type. Certain types of landscape are associated with particular rocks, and the evidence of mineral workings, drainage patterns, and vegetation can also be taken into account.

We sometimes speak of a rock being hard or soft, but of greater significance is its resistance to weathering, which is not the same thing. For example, chemical weathering may be more potent on a hard rock such as an old limestone than on a young rock such as clay which is also very soft. However, mechanical weathering will be more effective on the softer, younger rock. High and rugged ground is mostly built of resistant rocks such as granite, limestone and schists, whilst low-lying land is normally made of less resistant rocks such as clays and marls.

The permeability of a rock reflects the degree to which it allows water to pass through. The absence of surface drainage in this country indicates that the rock is highly permeable; this type of rock may be fissured, as in the case of an ancient limestone, or porous, as in the case of certain sandstones. In the latter case, water can percolate through the minute pores or spaces between the grains of the rock. On the other hand the presence of many streams or of marshland suggests that the rock is impermeable, which means that it does not allow water to pass through freely; slates, granite, and clays are examples.

**Drainage:** A description of the natural drainage of an area involves a study of the pattern of streams and rivers. There may be a complete absence of surface drainage as on much of the chalk land. Disappearing streams are a feature of markedly fissured rocks, for example Carboniferous Limestone. Marshland is a result of poorly drained land. Artificial drainage involves either the straightening of existing natural water courses or the digging of drainage ditches. The latter are normally distinguishable from streams by their straightness and right-angled bends.

In any description of the relief of an area, the main aim is to recognise the overall characteristics rather than the detailed description of individual small features. For example, you should talk in terms of an upland mass which is being dissected (or deeply cut into) by numerous incised streams; then reference may be made to particular examples of this.

**Rock types:**
(a) *Marl:* Keuper marl is a compacted limy clay. The white bands of anhydrite are a relic of dried-up salt lakes. Soils are retentive of moisture and support a good pasture.
(b) *Gravels:* A thick bed of unconsolidated, plateau gravels giving infertile soils supporting heather, gorse and bracken with mixed woodland.

(a)

(b)

(c) *Chalk :* Soft, permeable rock on which thin, dry soils support a short, tough grass much of which now is ploughed up for arable farming.

(e) *Carboniferous Limestone :* The thin soils on this permeable, well-jointed rock support a rough pasture for sheep and cattle.

(d) *Sandstone :* A young, loosely consolidated tertiary sandstone; highly permeable and of little agricultural value. Much natural vegetation of coarse grass and woodland remains.

(f) *Shales :* The bedrock is covered by a mantle of mainly shattered rock fragments which provide a poor soil on which a vegetation of bracken and heather develop. The land can be improved to form pasture for cattle and sheep.

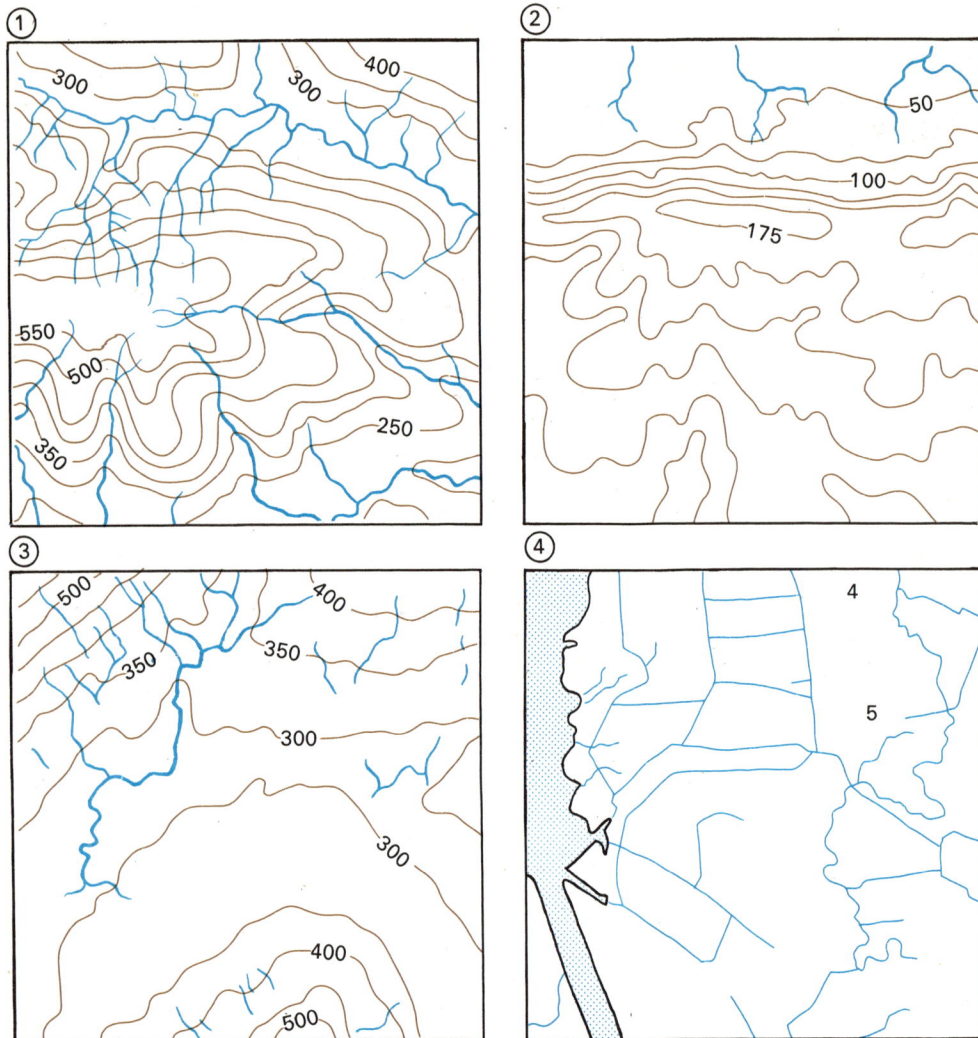

*Exercise :* Describe the drainage and relief shown on each of the four contour maps. Try to account for the characteristics you note. To help you, key words have been listed below but you will first need to pair these descriptions with the relevant map.

(a) Absence of drainage above 75m; dry valleys; rounded contours; scarp and dip; springs. Chalk downs near Arundel, Sussex.

(b) Discontinuous drainage; swallow holes; plateau; abrupt edges. Carboniferous Limestone of the Pennines near Settle.

(c) Drained plain; straight and winding watercourses; natural and artificial drainage. Fens near King's Lynn.

(d) Dissected upland; plateau top; numerous streams, some incised; skirting main valley. Millstone Grit and shales, High Peak in the South Pennines.

FIGURE 5

**Drainage patterns**

# SETTLEMENT

Settlement reflects the social, economic, and technical changes of the past four thousand years. Relics of late Stone Age settlements, which include hut circles, stone circles, and tumuli, are concentrated on upland areas of southern England particularly the Downs and Salisbury Plain, though much evidence has subsequently been removed by farming.

Settlement became more widespread with the development of a plough suited to the tilling of heavy clay soils. There followed a succession of invasions significantly adding to the size of the population. The Roman occupation provided little lasting effect on rural settlement, but their towns built in strategic locations and linked by efficient roadways have proved the sites for many of our cities of today. The place-name elements of -caster, -cester and -chester are most commonly associated with Roman occupation. The Anglo-Saxons and Scandinavians initially came as raiders and then settled. The Scandinavians restricted themselves to an area north and east of Watling Street. The place-name elements of -ton, -ing, -ington and ingham are possible indications of Anglo-Saxon settlement; -toft, -by, -garth and -booth are of Scandinavian origin.

**Site:** These early agricultural communities had to be self-sufficient. Their choice of site had to allow access to basic needs which included fresh water, fuel, building materials, arable and pastoral land; there was also a need for a firm foundation for the buildings. The site of a settlement is the spot on which it has grown up. This may be on a river bank or a spring-line if water was the major locational factor. Where security was the principal concern the settlement may have been sited on a gravel terrace or on a defensible hill top.

The site is sometimes indicated in the name of a settlement, as in the example used in figure 6. This small, nucleated village is built on what we call a 'dry-point' site, and this type is commonly found in the fen regions of Norfolk, Lincolnshire, and Cambridgeshire where protection from flooding was the major factor in determining the site. However evidence on the map indicates that such basic needs as water supply, timber, and farm land were available in the vicinity.

Figure 7 shows the settlement of Fulbeck lying at the foot of a scarp slope, on the banks of the Beck. The village is an example of a 'wet-point' site. *Describe in detail the site of Fulbeck.*

**Position:** The position of a settlement is its relationship with the surrounding area. It may be at the head of a valley, on a river estuary, or in the centre of a fertile river plain. Initially, communities had to be self-sufficient. Their population was limited by the resources of an area. The limits of the area serving the settlement is represented by the parish boundary. *Can you suggest why the parish boundaries of the two settlements illustrated in figures 6 and 7 are not the same size or shape?* Remember that parishes may have boundaries which take in both lowland pasture and upland rough grazing. The words 'fen', 'common', 'heath', and 'moor' sometimes indicate that the land has been reclaimed and added to the original parish.

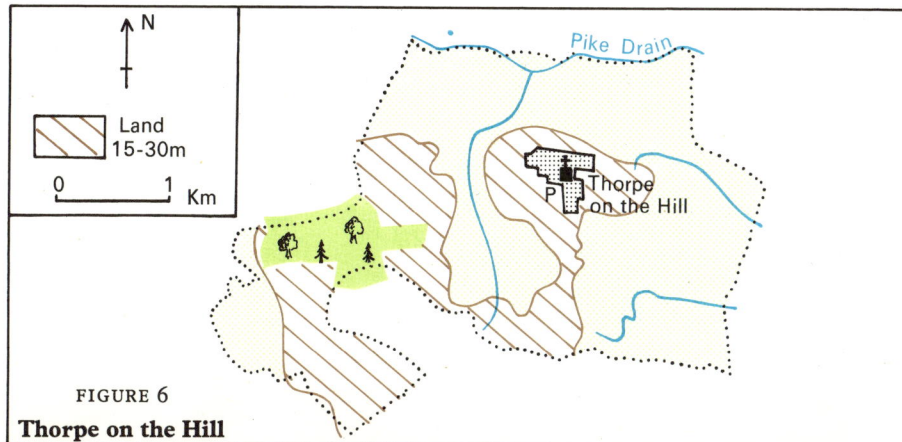

FIGURE 7
**Fulbeck**

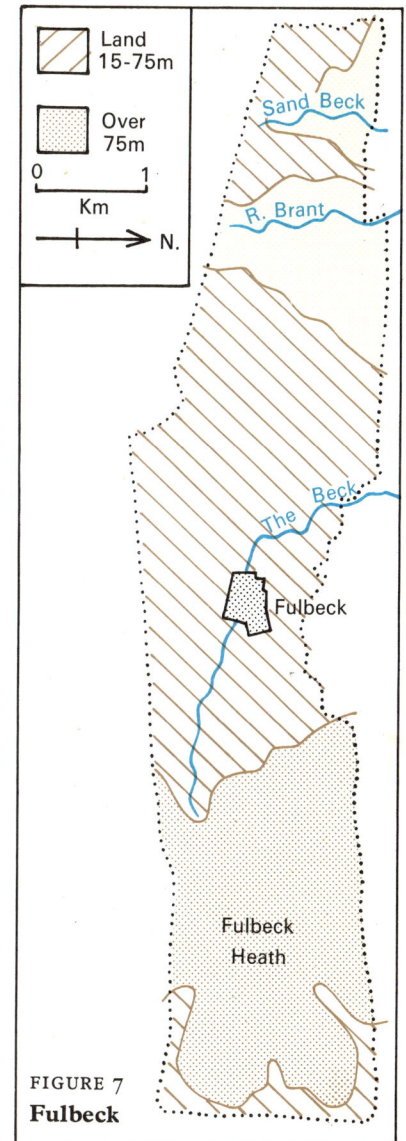

FIGURE 6
**Thorpe on the Hill**

*Exercise:* Draw a map of your own parish in a similar style to the maps of Thorpe on the Hill and Fulbeck. Compare the relief, size, shape, and drainage of all three parishes.

**Function:** The function of a settlement is concerned with what the inhabitants there do for a living and how it serves the surrounding area. This is not always clear from the study of a map. If we study the map of Thorpe on the Hill, apart from the shading denoting a few buildings, the church and the Post Office are the only distinctive features. We can suggest that the village probably functions as an agricultural village providing basic shopping facilities. A rural settlement with evidence of a housing estate may indicate that the village houses people employed in a nearby urban centre. The name of the settlement can sometimes assist in identifying its function, e.g. Market Harborough or Market Bosworth.

Coastal settlements frequently have obvious functions. The major ports have docks, warehouses, and railway sidings; resorts have promenades, beaches and sometimes piers; and ferry and packet stations may have the sea routes (indicating the services they run) marked. Industrial development can be indicated on a map by the word 'works', by large building blocks with railway sidings, and, in specialised cases, by the use of terms such as power station, mills, and steel works, or the symbol for oil containers. The nodality of a settlement may also be easy to distinguish; here we are assessing the settlement as a focus of routeways. Cathedrals and castles suggest a tourist function of the settlement. The size of a town is indicated by the style of lettering used for its name. It is likely that the bigger the size of the settlement the more varied will be its functions and also the more important are likely to be its commercial and entertainment facilities.

*Exercise :* Study the four maps which show different settlement patterns. Describe each pattern and explain how they differ.

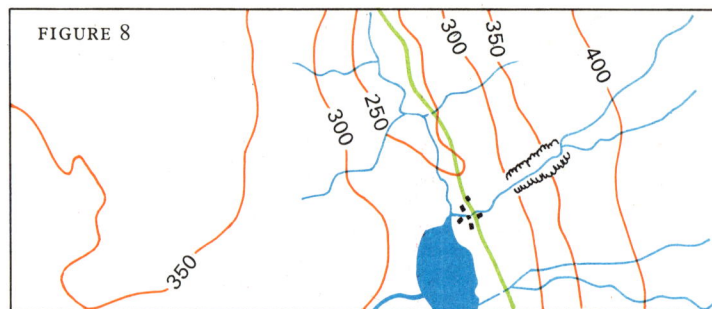

FIGURE 8

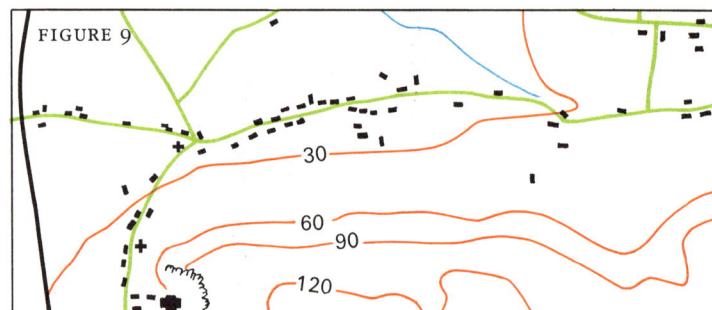

FIGURE 9

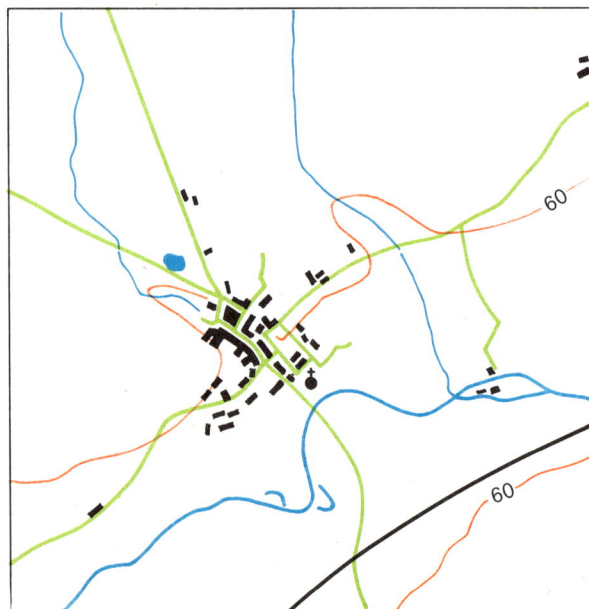

FIGURE 10

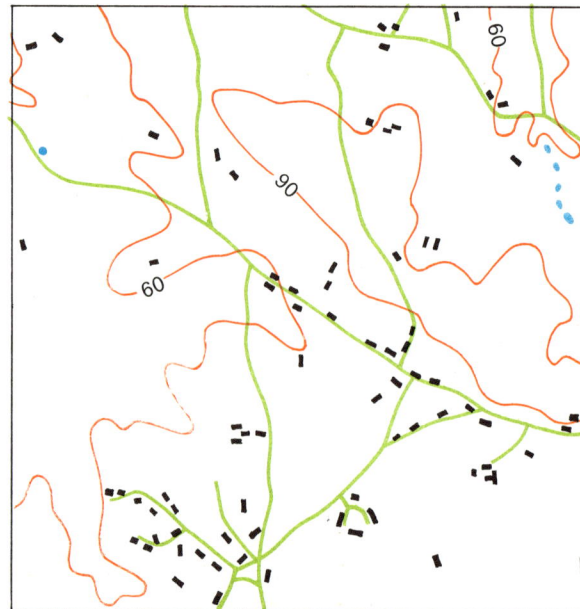

FIGURE 11

# SETTLEMENT PATTERNS

**The spacing of settlements:** Just as there is a relationship between the size and function of a settlement, so there is a relationship between the size and the spacing of different orders of settlement. Using an Ordnance Survey map one can recognise patterns by measuring the distances separating hamlets, villages, towns and cities. The table below shows how this has been done for settlement in West Leicestershire.

| Settlement | Average distance apart in km |
| --- | --- |
| City to town | 20·3 |
| Town to town | 12·0 |
| Town to village | 4·8 |
| Village to village | 3·3 |
| Village to hamlet | 2·9 |
| Hamlet to hamlet | 1·9 |

Although the average distances have been given in the above table, the actual measured distances varied only very slightly from the mean. Similar results have been obtained from measurements in chalk and fen country. Why should such a regular pattern emerge?

(1) The relief is level or gently undulating and there are no physical obstacles to settlement.

(2) The original self-sufficiency of the earliest settlements imposed a limit on the distance separating each settlement.

(3) Spacing has been governed by the mode of available transport. Local market centres established during the medieval period had to be within walking distance. As transport conditions have changed there has been a responding change in the spacing of settlements in newly developed areas, but at a slower rate. Relief will also affect the regularity of the pattern.

**Central Places:** Where settlements are regularly spaced and physical and agricultural conditions are uniform, the areas served by and serving each order of settlement should also be of uniform size and shape. If the 'tributary area' (service area) was circular this would mean that some land is not taken up (figure 12(a)) or the tributary areas would overlap (figure 12(b)). The most efficient shape that will not leave spaces nor overlap is a hexagon.

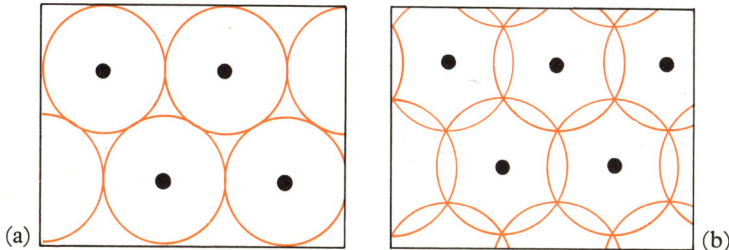

FIGURE 12

The hexagonal pattern of settlement distribution was recognised by Christaller, and can be applied to all orders of settlement.

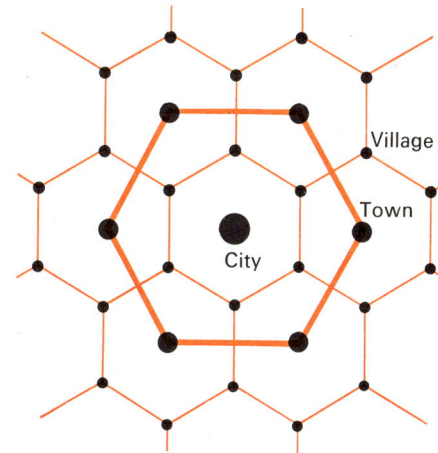

FIGURE 13

In applying this model to the settlement that we can observe on a map we must appreciate that uniform conditions of relief and agriculture do not always exist. Even so, it is frequently possible to recognise hexagonal patterns, and it is also significant when such patterns do not appear where we would most expect them.

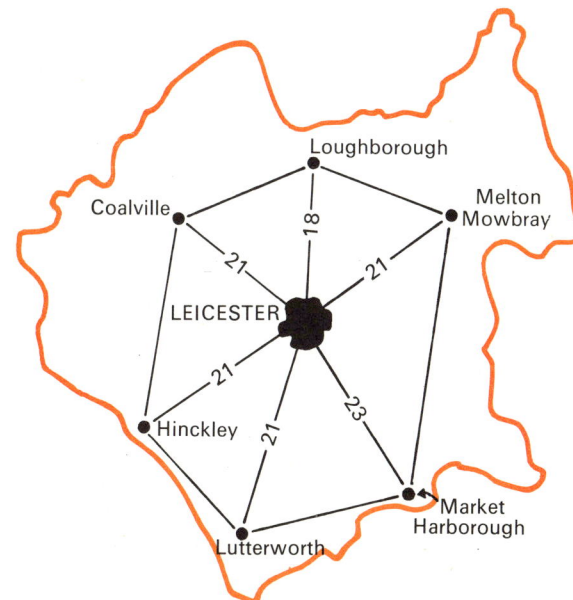

FIGURE 14

**The Leicestershire hexagon**

# COMMUNICATIONS

The term 'communications' can be applied to many types of links which serve man. They may be personal links by conversation or by the postal service. The mass media – television, radio, newspapers, and magazines – is a form of communication. In map reading, although we are primarily concerned with roads and railways, we should not ignore communications by sea, river, canal, air, pipeline, or transmission wires.

**Roads:** The pattern of roads has developed from prehistoric times. The first trackways we have any evidence of followed ridges above ill-drained marsh and thick woodland. Sites of antiquities now often mark the routes of these earliest lines of communication. The influence of the Romans upon our landscape is reflected in their legacy of road networks. Roads such as the Fosse Way and Watling Street, which linked military establishments, took straight paths despite physical obstacles. Considerably improved, these roads remain today as important links in our road network on account of their directness.

Subsequently roads have tended to avoid areas liable to flooding and areas where steep gradients are met. On a map it is possible to recognise cases where a road has been built on a river terrace above the flood plain, or where it takes a curved path following the contours of the hillside instead of a direct line along the steepest path. This attempt at 'ironing out' the relief is particularly apparent in motorway construction. These roads, designed for fast, long distance journeys have, at considerable cost, effectively used cuttings and embankments for this purpose.

On an ordnance survey map roads are classified according to their condition and function. Motorways by-pass towns which are linked to them by feeder roads. 'A' class roads normally link towns, whereas 'B' roads, which are of secondary importance, frequently join towns with larger villages. Unclassified roads have a more local function.

**Railways:** The Ordnance Survey map distinguishes four types of railway line – (a) multiple and (b) single tracks of the standard gauge, (c) narrow gauge and (d) mineral lines, sidings or tramways. Railways are concentrated in industrial areas or corridors linking centres of population. Their routes are to a greater degree con-trolled by relief than are those for roads because most railway engines are unable to operate over steep gradients. Where railways are unable to follow valleys or coastal plains, cuttings, embankments and viaducts have often been necessary; where cuttings were insufficient to provide a route across an upland, tunnels were dug out.

Figure 15 illustrates how little traffic the railways now carry compared with roads. There may be evidence of this on a map; closed stations and abandoned lines are often marked; these show the attempts to economise by the closure of unprofitable branch lines and little-used stations.

*Exercise:* Comment on the routes of the multiple railway lines shown on the Medway extract.

**Rivers:** It is not always possible to discover the extent to which rivers serve as lines of communication. Certainly many were once far more important than they are today. However, with the size of ships increasing and the more efficient alternatives to river transport being developed, rivers and riverside docks have tended often to fall into disuse. Reference to wharves, locks and other installations may provide evidence that the river is or has been used by certain types of craft.

**Canals:** Although some canals are still used by barges carrying bulky goods, most are used only by pleasure craft today. Their construction during the early stages of the industrial revolution was made possible only by the use of aqueducts, embankments, cuttings, and tunnels to obtain a level course, and locks to enable movement from one level to another.

**Air Communications:** Although air routes are not shown, airports which act as passenger terminals are named and airfields which are used by the Air Force or clubs are similarly marked as such. Runways for aircraft are indicated by broken lines. They need to be sited on flat ground and, because of the space they require and the noise produced, they are usually sited some distance from built-up areas.

**Description of a route:** In a description of a route, reference should be made to distance, direction, elevation, slope, and the nature of the landforms crossed. You should discuss the ways in which the route negotiates natural obstacles such as steep gradients, flood plains, and watercourses by such means as tunnels, cuttings, bridges, and embankments.

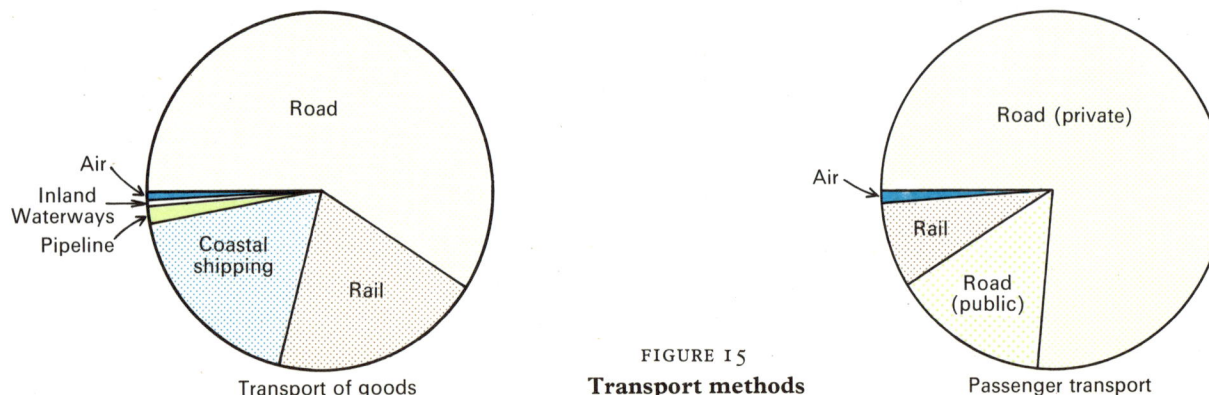

Air
Inland Waterways
Pipeline
Coastal shipping
Rail
Road

Transport of goods

FIGURE 15
**Transport methods**

Air
Rail
Road (private)
Road (public)

Passenger transport

# ACCESSIBILITY

## The accessibility of places in a network
The efficiency of communications depends upon the ease of access to places within a network.

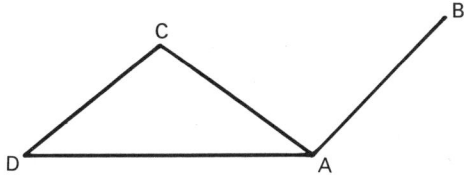

FIGURE 16

In the above figure which shows a network of communications, A is the most accessible point because you can reach B, C or D by means of a single journey. To reach D and C from B involves two journeys. We use the word 'link' to describe the journey between two places. The number of links needed to reach the furthest point in the network by the shortest route is called the accessibility number.

**Example.** To discover which is the most accessible, Hinckley or Leicester.

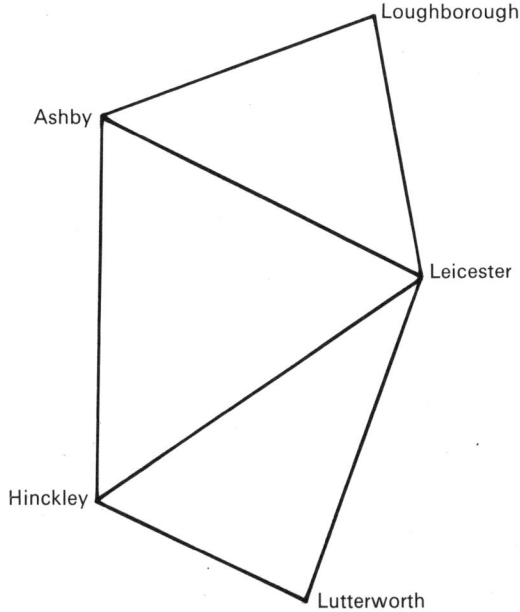

FIGURE 17

Calculations

| Accessibility number for Hinckley | Links | | Accessibility number for Leicester | Links |
|---|---|---|---|---|
| Hinckley to Loughborough | 2 | | Leicester to Loughborough | 1 |
| to Ashby | 1 | | to Ashby | 1 |
| to Leicester | 1 | | to Hinckley | 1 |
| to Lutterworth | 1 | | to Lutterworth | 1 |

Therefore the accessibility number for Hinckley is 2.

Therefore the accessibility number for Leicester is 1.

Therefore Leicester is more accessible than Hinckley.

*Exercise:* Calculate the accessibility of Ashby and Loughborough in this network.

## The accessibility of a network
In Britain, communications have, until recently, developed in a haphazard manner. In areas where there are few links already in existence it is possible to devise a network in order to give the maximum accessibility. At the same time one can also comment upon the accessibility of existing networks.

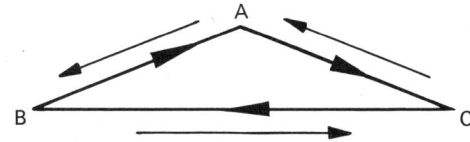

FIGURE 18.

In the above example there are 6 possible links. This is the number of places in the network multiplied by this number less one. (Only two journeys can be made from any one place.) As each link is duplicated the formula for the maximum number of links is given by:

$$\frac{\text{(Number of places)} \times \text{(Number of places less 1)}}{2}$$

Therefore the maximum number of links is $\frac{6}{2}$ or 3.

If you compare the maximum number of links with the actual number of links in the network you can calculate the accessibility of the network.

Accessibility is $\dfrac{\text{Maximum number of links}}{\text{Actual number of links}}$ which is $\dfrac{3}{3}$ or 1.

This is the most accessible network of all.

**Example.** In figure 17 five places are linked in the network. Therefore the maximum accessibility is $\frac{5 \times 4}{2}$ or 10. The actual number of links is 7. The accessibility of the network is $\frac{10}{7}$ or 1·43.

*Photograph Aerofilms Ltd*

# QUESTIONS ON THE MEDWAY MAP

**Exercise A**

1. (a) What material was quarried in this area? Give map references for your evidence.
   (b) Why are there few surface streams shown on the map?
   (c) What type of relief feature is in square 7664?
2. Give six figure references to locate the beacons in the mouth of the estuary of the Medway. Why are they there?
3. Draw a plan of the section of the motorway which appears on the map. Mark on this plan all the features associated with the motorway (e.g. sliproads, cuttings, bridges, viaducts). Label these features.
4. What problems were encountered by the constructors of the M2 judging from the evidence on your plan?

**Exercise B**

1. Describe the character of the estuary downstream from Sun Pier at 755682. Use evidence which appears either on the map or the photograph.
2. Construct an annotated section from Gibraltar Farm (779633) to 800690. Mark on your section built-up areas, main and secondary roads, woodlands and orchards.
3. Comment on the land use along the line of your section. Is there any correlation between relief and land use?
4. Describe the location of the built-up areas and then make a list of the factors which account for this location.

**Essay Work**

On a map of the British Isles mark the course of all the motorways. Label each of them.

What effect have motorways had (a) in easing congestion on our roads and (b) in giving access to previously remote areas?

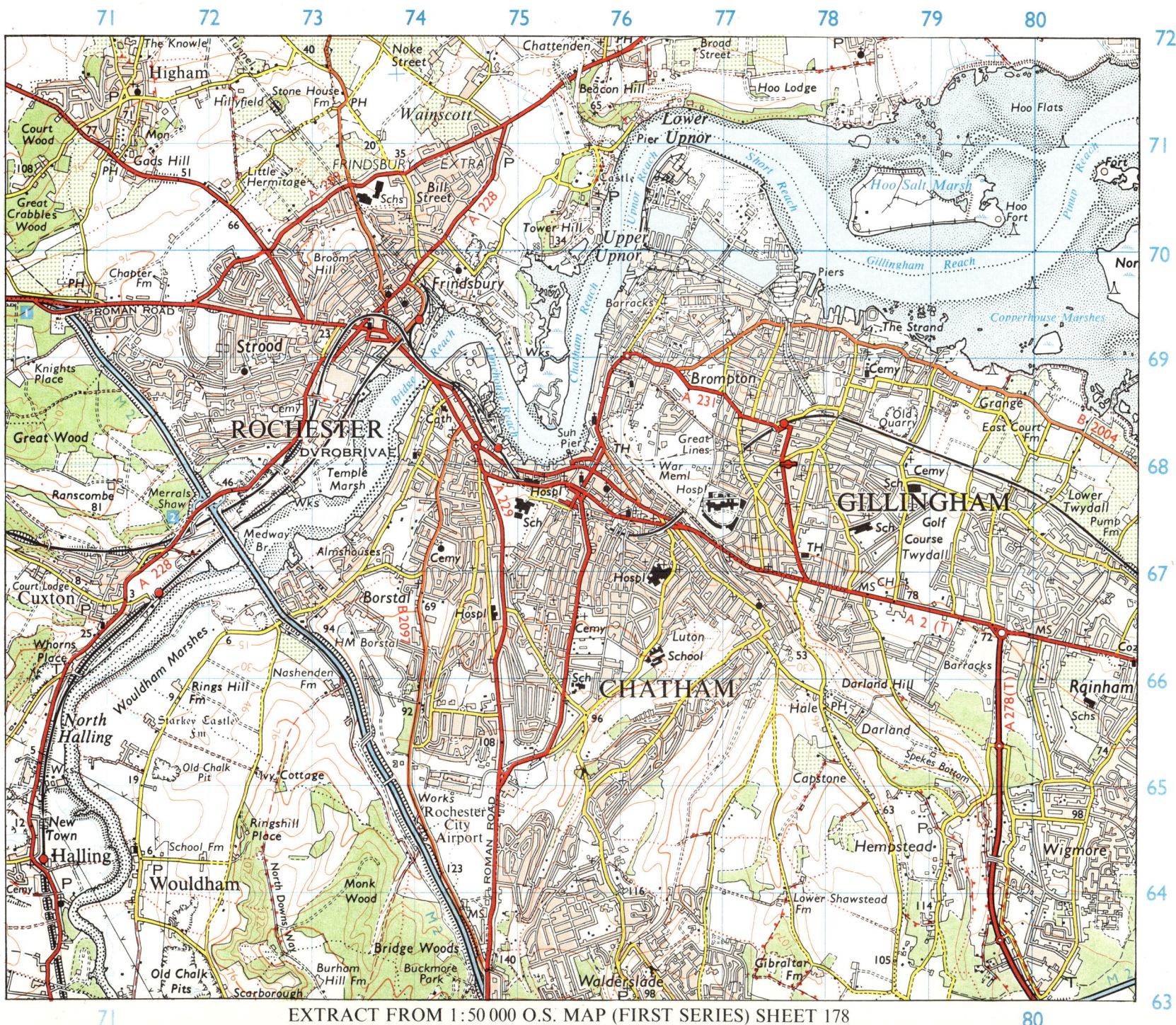

EXTRACT FROM 1:50 000 O.S. MAP (FIRST SERIES) SHEET 178

**Chalk Scenery:** Chalk is one of the most easily recognised rock types. It is a soft, white limestone and has minute pores and thread-like fractures or cracks so that water passes through very slowly. For example, a boring into chalk may take many days to fill with water although the borehole goes below the water table into water-saturated rock. Nevertheless, the rock is sufficiently permeable that chalk uplands are generally devoid of surface drainage. However, rivers do cut across chalk uplands maintaining a course which was taken long before the present relief pattern evolved; they do so in deep valleys which form gaps through the chalk uplands.

Most of the British chalk uplands take the form of cuestas; these have a steep slope, sometimes known as the scarp or escarpment, and a gentle or dip slope. The overall relief outline is one of smooth, rounded curves with convex slopes dominating. The dry valleys are a feature of chalk country; those that cut into the scarp slope are short and steep sided with an abrupt upper end, and are called coombes in some parts of the country. On the dip slope, the dry valleys are longer and shallower with tributary valleys leading off. Temporary streams, known as bournes or winterbournes, may flow in the 'dry' valleys for some months of the year when the water table is high. The water table, which is the upper level of saturation of a permeable rock, will be higher after a wet spell of weather. At the foot of both the scarp and the dip can be traced a spring line; this is normally at the junction of the chalk with underlying impermeable rocks.

Soil that develops on chalk is thin and is covered with a short, tough grass with occasional areas where box and yew grow. Also on some chalk areas there are clumps of beech; these have shallow roots which radiate out for considerable distances. Until recent years, chalk lands were used almost exclusively for pasture, particularly for sheep. Where surface water is limited, small round ponds known as dew ponds are numerous; some of these are natural but many are lined with concrete. These watering points for livestock are also numerous in other limestone areas. Today, the gentler slopes are regularly cropped, although both cattle and sheep are grazed on the leys. Farms are large, extending often to over 500 hectares, and barley is the chief crop. The soil is naturally of low fertility so that considerable use is made of fertilisers.

Chalk uplands are very thinly settled, villages developing on the spring line. Larger villages and towns tend to develop at gaps in the chalk.

**Clay Scenery:** Clay is a finely grained, soft rock which is easily eroded and very retentive of moisture. It does not have joints or bedding planes and once it is saturated it is impervious. Claylands are normally undulating lowlands with much surface drainage. Rivers meander and are likely to build up alluvial coatings near their banks due to periodic flooding; here the relief will be very flat, the borders often being marked by river terraces.

The claylands were once either covered with thick, deciduous woodland, oak and elm being the dominant species, or, where drainage was poor, they were waterlogged marshy areas. Over the centuries these lands have been drained and cleared, and now, although hedgerows give a well-wooded appearance to the countryside, mere copses are the remaining relics. The heavy soils which develop on the clay are more expensive and difficult to prepare for arable crops than light soils, but they do support a rich grass. Consequently these areas tend to be mixed farming regions, individual farmers specialising perhaps on beef production, dairying, sheep farming or, less often, on crops. Settlements avoid the lower-lying areas, but frequent village sites are slight elevations such as gravel pockets and terraces.

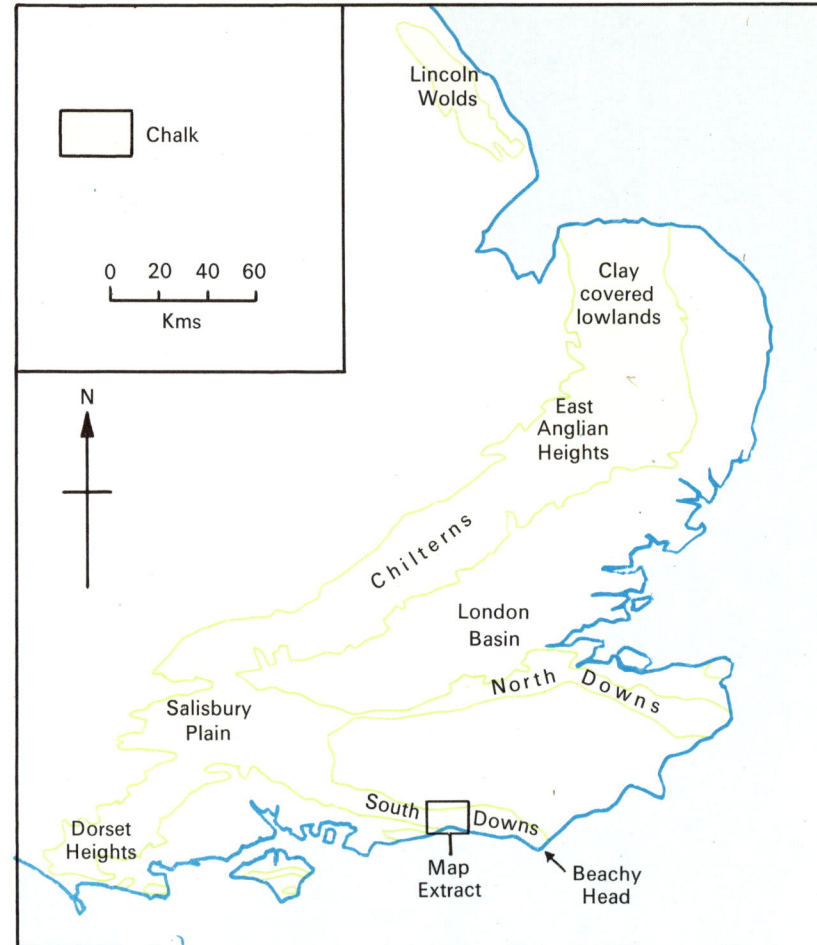

FIGURE 19
**Chalklands of South and East England**

**The Shoreham Area:** The map extract over the page is of a portion of the South Downs in Sussex together with a coastal plain immediately to the west of Brighton. *First read the general account on chalk scenery and then consider the following clues which may indicate that the area on a map is chalk. Individually, these clues are certainly not necessarily conclusive.*

Cement works (also in other limestone areas), chalk pits, place names ending in coombe or bourne, white horses cut in the rock, many references to tumuli and barrows (but these are found on many other open uplands), the terms 'down' in south-east England and 'wold' in Yorkshire and Lincolnshire, normally a complete absence of surface drainage but many dry valleys, dew ponds.

*Next, study the map extract and identify the upland area and then find eight clues which, taken together, prove that the uplands are made of chalk.*

North of the Chalk scarp lies the Vale of Sussex. Only a small portion of this appears on the extract, but there is sufficient for you to identify an area of undulating lowland which has been produced by the wearing down, mainly by running water, of the relatively soft, impermeable clay. Nearer the River Adur, in this northern portion of the map extract, the scenery is different; the land is much flatter, artificial drainage is needed, and there is a considerable stretch where there is an absence of settlement. *Read again the general account on clay scenery and then explain why there is this difference between the undulating land and the flatter tract in the Vale of Sussex.*

South of the South Downs lies a fertile coastal plain formed on alluvial and other recent deposits. It was formerly noted for market gardening including the hothouse cultivation of vegetables and flowers. Is there any evidence on the extract that this activity still exists? The spread of housing has converted a number of separate towns, including Brighton, Shoreham, and Worthing, into a sprawling coastal conurbation. In the main this is a residential and holiday area.

*Shoreham harbour* lies behind a shingle spit which grew eastwards across the estuary of the River Adur as a result of the west to east longshore drift. Sand and mud accumulated on the landward side, and in the course of time salt marshes were formed. In 1760 the entrance to the port was at Aldrington at the eastern end of the present harbour. Shortly afterwards a cut was made in the shingle spit farther to the west. A second cut was made in 1821 on the site of the present harbour entrance.

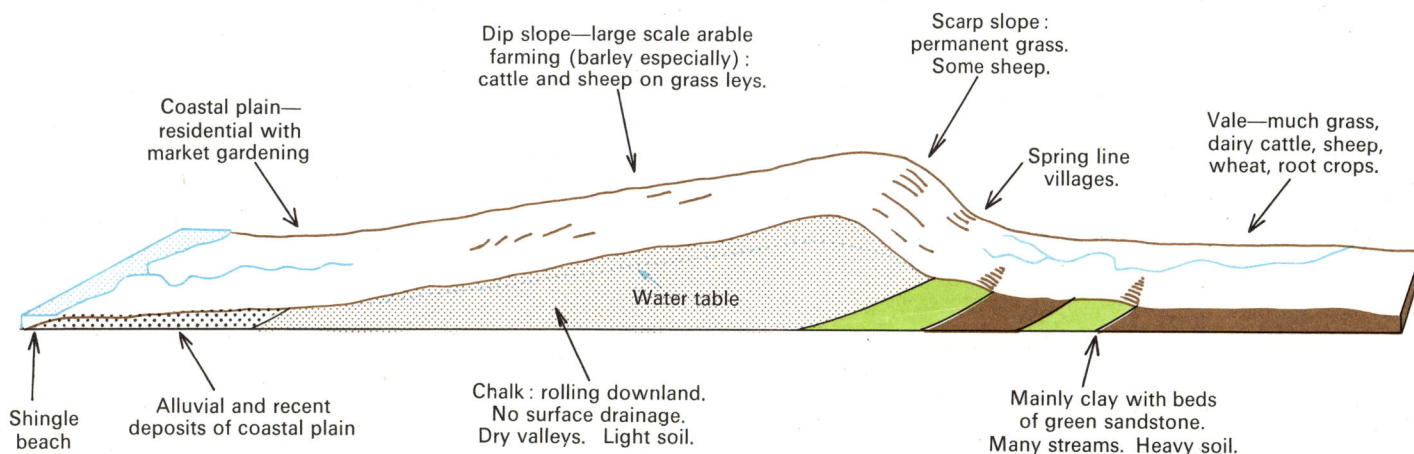

Coastal plain— residential with market gardening

Dip slope—large scale arable farming (barley especially): cattle and sheep on grass leys.

Scarp slope: permanent grass. Some sheep.

Spring line villages.

Vale—much grass, dairy cattle, sheep, wheat, root crops.

Water table

Shingle beach

Alluvial and recent deposits of coastal plain

Chalk: rolling downland. No surface drainage. Dry valleys. Light soil.

Mainly clay with beds of green sandstone. Many streams. Heavy soil.

FIGURE 20

**Section across the South Downs**

*Photograph Aerofilms Ltd*

# QUESTIONS ON THE SHOREHAM MAP

## Exercise A

1. Which of the following land forms – plain, dry valley, scarp, gap, spur – is to be found at 262075, 265112, 200055, 235112, 200080?
2. Quote, giving grid references, TWO pieces of evidence for prehistoric life.
3. You meet a motorist at Fulking (248115) who asks you the way to Bramber Castle (185107). He has no map or compass. Draw a simple sketch map of the route he requires, containing the necessary directions.
4. Describe the view from the triangulation pillar at 212078 looking west and comment on the routes followed by the roads.

## Photograph question

After you have studied the photograph carefully make two lists. On the first list include the information which a photograph shows but which a map cannot; on the second list give the information that the map shows but which a photograph cannot.

## Exercise B

1. Draw a map of the area covered by the Shoreham extract but on a scale of 1 : 100 000 to show a division of the area into three geographical regions. Name the three regions, insert the 76m contour, the River Adur, and print the words SCARP SLOPE and DIP SLOPE in the correct places.
2. Describe the distribution and type of settlement in each of the three regions you have marked. Study the section on the previous page and then explain how the physical geography has influenced the settlement.
3. Describe the physical features of the River Adur and its valley from Bramber to the sea.
4. Comment on the presence of (a) a castle at 185107, (b) a golf course in 2610 and (c) locks at 242048.

## Essay Work

Draw a map to show the chalk outcrops of England and, with the aid of your atlas, name as many of the hills formed of chalk as possible. Also name any clay vales that you can find.

What are the main differences between chalk and clay in respect of the nature of the rock and the physical and human features of the landscapes?

# HULL

**The development of Hull as a port:** There was a port at the mouth of the River Hull in 1160. In 1280 it was acquired by Edward I, renamed Kingston-upon-Hull, and it soon became the third port of the kingdom. It remained a river port based upon the estuary of the Hull river until 1809, when the Humber Dock which opened directly onto the Humber came into use.

The Hull estuary had provided a sheltered site with ample quay space for the small craft of the middle ages. On the other hand, the land here was subject to flooding and much of the surrounding area was marsh. With the early stages of the Industrial Revolution midway through the eighteenth century, there was a much greater demand on the port of Hull for here was a point where the larger ocean-going vessels could transfer goods to the narrow canal boats for transport up the Aire–Calder systems to the new industrial regions of the West Riding of Yorkshire.

The first docks to be dug out from the soft clays and alluvium followed the line of the old outer wall and moat which had protected the old city; these were Queens, Princes, and Humber Docks. By 1850 much larger docks were needed to cope with the trade created by the nearby industrial regions of the West Riding and Midlands, and great expanses of the unoccupied marshy land to the east and west of the old city were taken. To the east, Victoria Dock was constructed, while to the west a long line of docks was formed by excavating enormous trenches, the material re-moved being used to build up a secure embankment between the docks and the Humber estuary. The more recent expansion has continued downstream of the city centre. The largest docks system is the King George with its recent extension, the Queen Elizabeth; the three kilometres of quayside in this dock complex includes new and extensive facilities for container and vehicle traffic.

*Exercise:* Read this short account on the development of Hull as a port and study the maps. Then explain the advantages and disadvantages which have influenced Hull's development. Consider both features of site (there are at least three) and also position in relation to hinterland and direction of overseas trade.

**Hull as a manufacturing centre:** The main manufacturing industries of Hull developed where imported raw materials could be readily obtained from the docks. Therefore the sites of these manufacturing concerns have concentrated alongside the docks in a belt some ten kilometres long while another belt extends on either side of the River Hull for some four kilometres. The finished products of these factories include margarine, soap, glue, rice, fish meal and fertilisers, flour, paint, and chipboard. *What raw materials are required for these factories and where would these products be imported from?*

There are new industrial pockets on the outer fringes of the city. To the east the Salt End industrial estate uses the oil and other liquids piped ashore into the depots there for the manufacture of chemicals, plastics, and textile fibres. Other new industrial concerns also provide alternatives to the earlier concentration on the processing of imported vegetable products to give a broader manufacturing base; they are concerned with light engineering and clothing products.

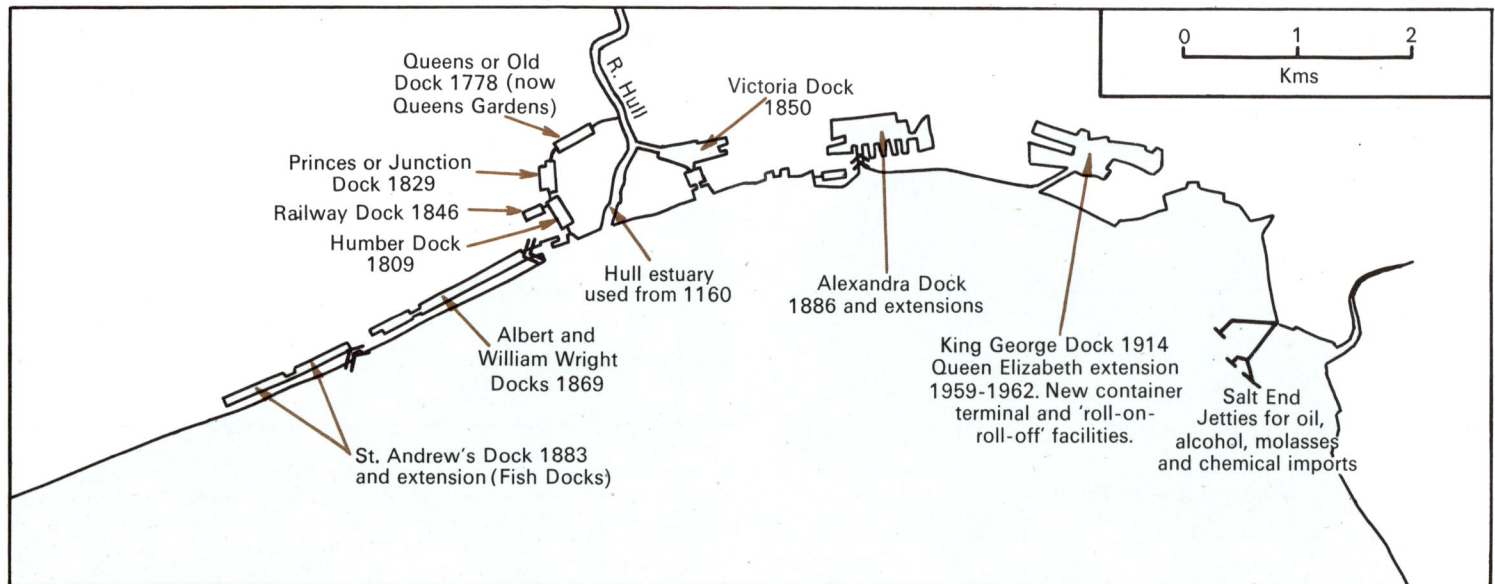

FIGURE 21
**Hull Docks**

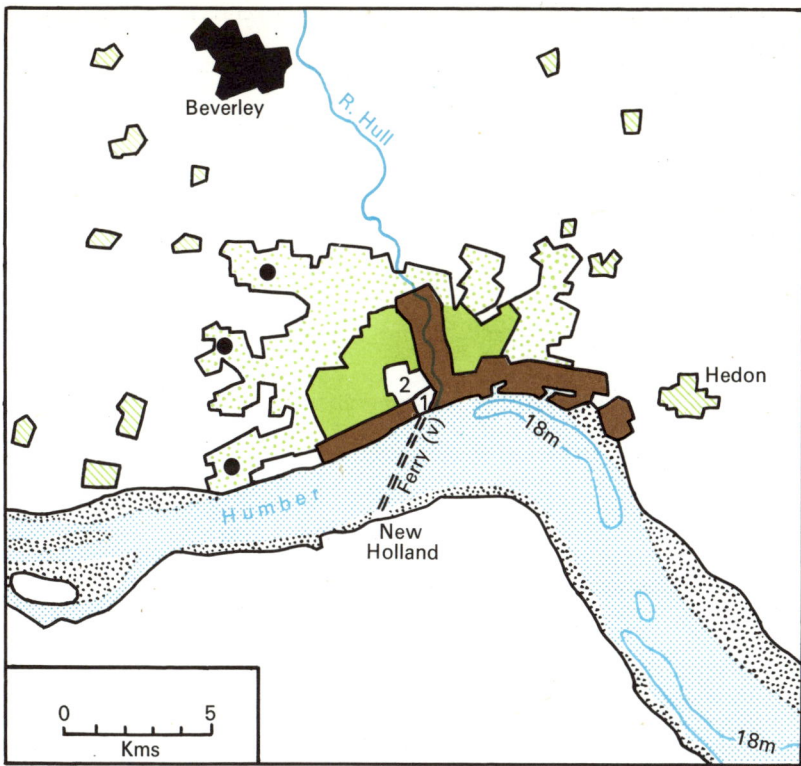

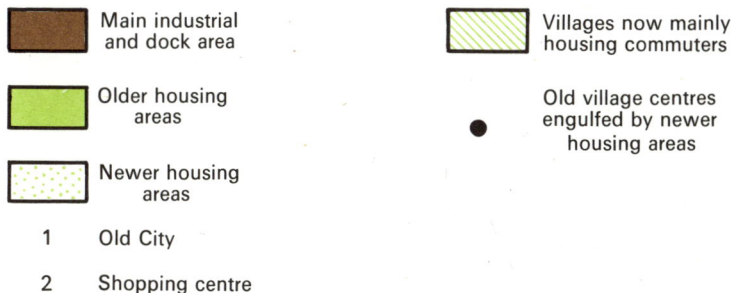

FIGURE 22
**The structure of Hull**

*Legend:*

Main industrial and dock area

Older housing areas

Newer housing areas

Villages now mainly housing commuters

Old village centres engulfed by newer housing areas

1 Old City

2 Shopping centre

**The settlement patterns of Hull:** Normally, one cannot positively identify types of settlement from an ordnance survey extract, but the evidence available can give pointers to the types that may have developed.

*Exercise :* Study the five patterns illustrated in figure 23 and then attempt to identify these from the extract. Suggest other patterns on the extract which are similar and give the references. The simplified structure plan of Hull should help.

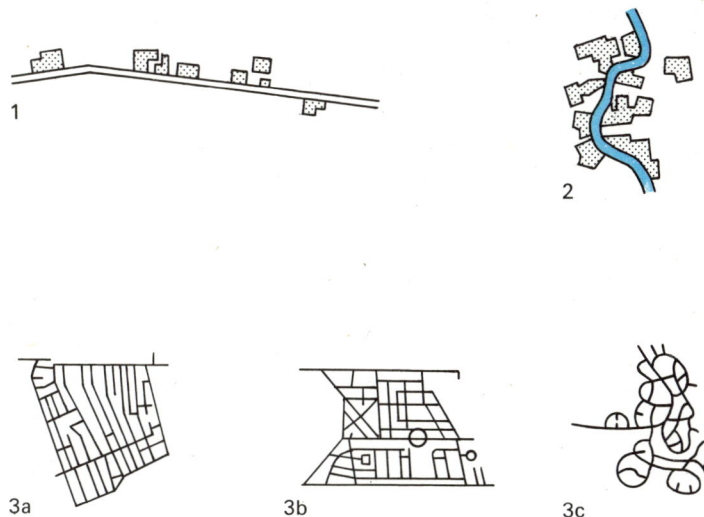

FIGURE 23
**Settlement patterns in Hull**

(1) Ribbon-like industrial development which can use the services of the adjoining main road together with the dock facilities the other side of the road.

(2) Similar large blocks but this time served by railways and extending alongside the River Hull which provides barge quayage on the plant's site.

(3) Various residential patterns. In these three diagrams only the road pattern is indicated.
   (a) Many long lines of streets; rectangular, gridiron pattern; near to the city centre and the older docks. This suggests the long-established housing areas.
   (b) Geometrical patterns, very ordered and balanced, consisting of squares, diagonals, and circles; located on or near the edge of the city. These suggest integrated, planned housing areas; the unimaginative patterns are typical of many housing estates built in the period 1930 to 1950.
   (c) Flowing, rounded, irregular road patterns with crescents and cul-de-sacs forming compact residential areas of the type found on the edge of many large towns; generally constructed since 1950.

*Photograph Aerofilms Ltd*

# QUESTIONS ON THE KINGSTON-UPON-HULL MAP

**Exercise A**

1. (a) Give six figure references for the main railway station and the Hull terminus of the vehicle ferry.
   (b) Identify the symbols at 164268 and 118312.
2. (a) Identify four types of road in square 1432 and then illustrate and label each of them.
   (b) Identify three types of railway in square 1329 and then illustrate and label each of them.
3. Using only the evidence on the map, give as many reasons as you can which help to suggest the purpose of the enclosed water space at 145287.
4. Compare the watercourse which runs south from 083340 with that running south from 127340. In what ways do they differ?

**Practical Work**

Identify the area covered by the photograph on the map extract. Then draw a plan of the area covered by the photograph marking on it the docks, dockside warehouses and probable factory and housing areas.

**Exercise B**

1. Study the settlement patterns in the vicinities of 070330, 080280, and 118293. One is an industrial block, one an old housing area, and one a new housing estate. Pair the descriptions with the grid references and give reasons why you do so.
2. Study the human development in square 1627. Then, using the evidence on the map only, describe the complex and explain why it might be located there.
3. Describe the general pattern of rail communications on the map. What changes have taken place recently? What reasons can you give for your observations.
4. Account for the location of the sand banks exposed at low tide.

**Essay Work**

Write an account on the fishing industry of Britain paying particular attention to the part played by Kingston-upon-Hull in this industry.

# KINGSTON UPON HULL

West Carr

Haworth Hall

Frog Hall Fm

Field

Course of old railway

Turmer Hall

Hungerhills

Bilton

GHAM

New age

Carr Ho

Golf Course

Sutton-on-Hull

CH

Infmy

MS

Swan Hill

Moat

B 1238

University

Newland

Stoneferry

Sutton Ings

Tilworth Grange

Cemy

East Park

Summergangs

Somerden Ho

Longsight

West Fm

Sculcoates

Cemy

Sch

Hospl

Cemy

Cemy

Sch

Marfleet

The Limes

West Park

HM Prison

Cemy

Hospl

Infmy

A 1033

Grange Fm

MP

Salt End Jetties

Pau

Ferry

R I V E R

H

Goxhill Haven

Skitter Ness

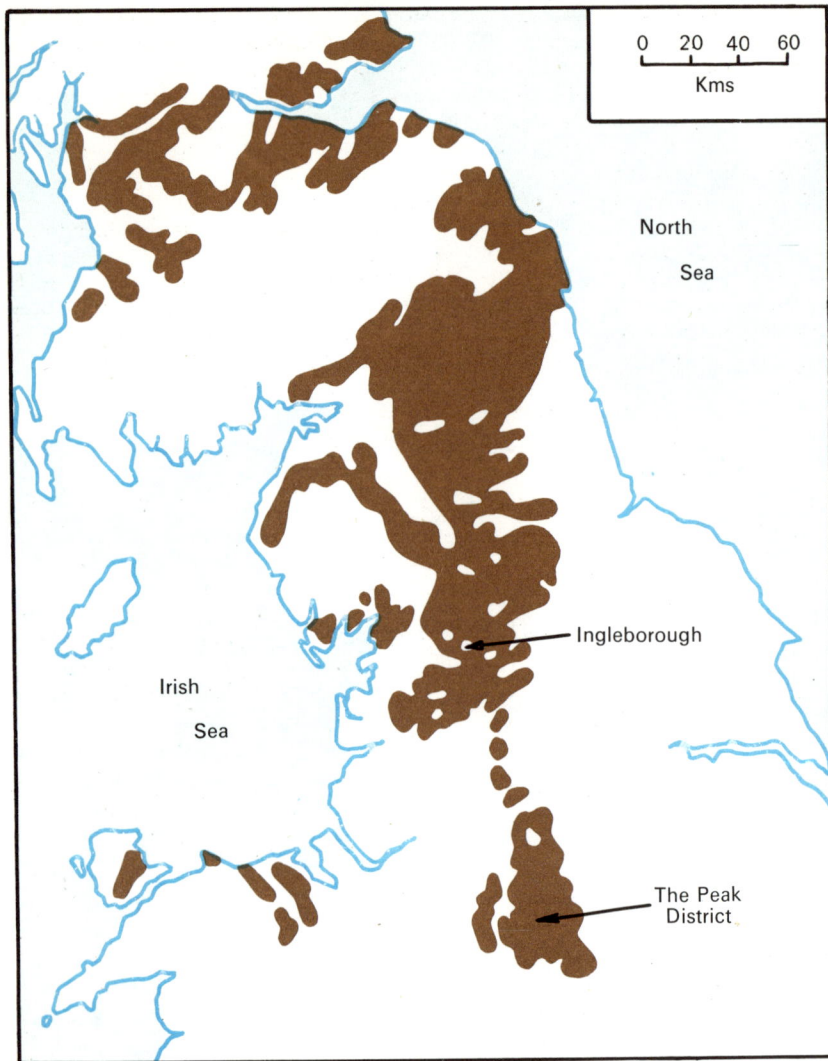

FIGURE 24

**Carboniferous limestone areas of Northern England**

# INGLEBOROUGH

**Carboniferous Limestone Scenery:** The Carboniferous Limestone series in Great Britain is over 1000 metres thick but not all of this is limestone. In the series, beds of limestone are interspersed with layers of less resistant shales and sandstones. The limestone itself has well-developed systems of joints and bedding plants and is consequently permeable. It is very resistant to mechanical weathering but chemical weathering plays a significant part in the development of limestone scenery. Rainwater absorbs carbon dioxide from the air to become a very dilute carbonic acid which reacts on the limestone, carrying away small quantities of calcium carbonate in solution. This process has an obvious effect where limestone beds are thick; here watercourses follow fissures in the rock, enlarging them and creating a labyrinth of underground watercourses many of which have been subsequently abandoned.

The limestone uplands provide a rolling, plateau-like landscape. The upper surface is devoid of drainage but rivers occupying deep troughs have cut the uplands into blocks. Even shallow dry valleys frequently are bordered by precipitous edges of limestone. The open, light appearance of the uplands is due partly to the absence of trees and partly to the light grey colour of the weathered rock where it outcrops as scars or pavements. In the areas used for farming, this appearance is heightened by the dry stone walling surrounding the many small fields.

The thin soils of the uplands support a coarse grass which provides adequate pasture for the hardy, upland breeds of sheep. In contrast, the steep valleysides are sometimes thickly wooded. Villages are normally located in the valleys, but the plateau surface over much of the limestone country is dotted by isolated farms often sited in shallow hollows. Where the valleys are deep and winding, roads tend to avoid them, keeping rather to the plateau, but where the rivers have opened up wide vales a typical communication pattern of twin roads, each close to one side of the vale, has emerged. *Why do you think this is so? Consider winding rivers, cost of bridge construction, water meadows, and the location of farms built on dry sheltered sites close to springs.*

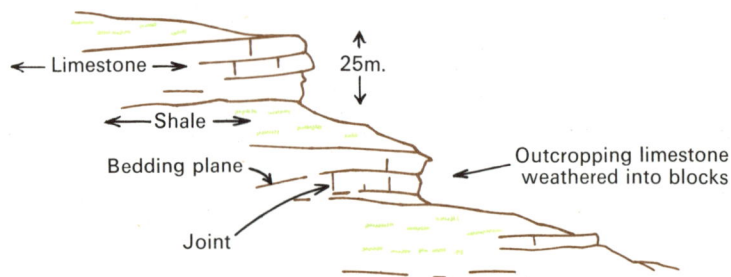

FIGURE 25

**Field sketch of an outcrop of Yoredales**

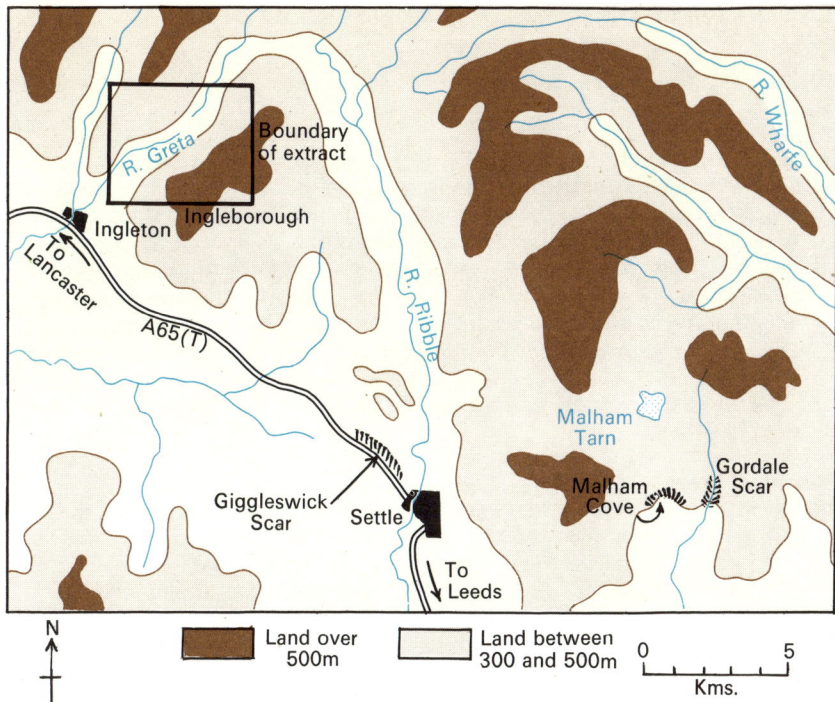

FIGURE 26

**The Central Pennines**

**The Ingleborough Area.** The Ingleborough extract illustrates many of the features of Carboniferous Limestone. The crest of Ingleborough is capped with a layer of Millstone Grit, but most of the steep slopes immediately below this capping are made up of a series of rocks called Yoredales. These consist of repeated bands of limestone, shales, and sandstone which give a stepped appearance, the limestone outcrop forming the scar and the less resistant shales and sandstones forming the bench as is illustrated in the field sketch. This type of outcrop is typical of much of the limestone scenery throughout the Pennines.

Below the Yoredale slope there is a great shelf of massive limestone which forms a plateau just above 400 metres high. This particular layer of rock is known as Great Scar Limestone and its outer edge forms precipitous scars which provide vertical or near vertical drops of over 150 metres in places. The joints are very marked and the layer is uninterrupted by other impermeable beds. Consequently, streams running down from the upper rocks, when they reach this shelf, soon plunge into swallow holes some of which are vertical drops of up to 120 metres. The streams emerge at the surface lower down just above the impermeable, older rocks on which the limestone rests. These older rocks have been exposed by erosion in the valley floor of the River Greta.

The Pennines were covered by ice sheets during the Ice Age, and although there are not such obvious features of glaciation here as in the mountainous areas of the country, nevertheless many of the major Pennine vales, including that of the Greta, have been deepened by ice action.

*Exercise :* Now that you have read the general account on limestone scenery and the specific account on the Ingleborough area, study the map extract of the area. Then consider the following clues which may indicate that portions of the extract are made of Carboniferous Limestone. List those which apply, giving grid references.

Disappearing streams; collapsed caverns; gorges; the use of terms such as swallets, swallow holes, potholes, and scars; limestone quarries and lime works (also present in other limestone areas); dew ponds (particularly numerous in farmed areas of the Carboniferous Limestone).

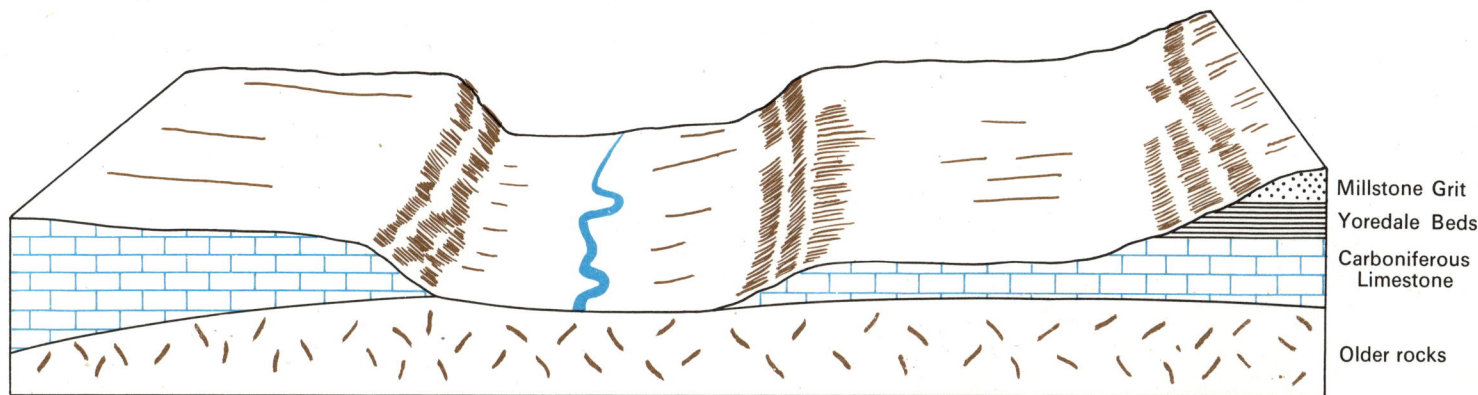

FIGURE 27

**Section across the Greta Valley**

25

# QUESTIONS ON THE INGLEBOROUGH MAP

### Exercise A

1. What is the land surface like at (a) 735755, (b) 730771, (c) 744764?
2. Give a detailed description of the River Greta and its valley. The following suggestions may help. Is the valley wide or narrow? How wide? At what point? What is the relief of the valley floor and how steep are its sides (for example there may be a gradient equivalent to an ascent of 300m in 1km)? Is the river fast flowing? Does it wind or meander? Are the tributaries lengthy? Which way does the river flow? How does the valley differ in square 7377 from 7175?
3. Describe the courses of the two roads in relation to the relief and drainage courses.
4. Give the grid references which indicate three different human activities practised in the area.

### Practical Work

On a grid showing all the eastings and northings and on the same scale as the extract, mark in the 900-foot and 1800-foot contours and all the drainage systems shown. Between what levels do you find surface drainage and between what levels is there no evidence of surface drainage? What can you deduce from this?

### Exercise B

1. Draw an accurate section along the line from 710780 to 750740. Mark on it the River Greta, Ingleborough Hill, and any scars crossed.
2. Along the line of the section calculate the degree of slope at certain stages to illustrate changes in the relief. For example, you might take (a) the slope on Great Hard Rigg Moss between the footpath and the top of the scar, (b) the slope from the top of the scars to the road near Sprincote, and (c) the slope from 738750 to the platform edge of Ingleborough.
3. Describe the general features of the relief of the map using the evidence of your section and calculations of slopes.
4. Under what circumstances do you find the following features: scars, pot holes (of the type mentioned on the map extract), caves, springs, and mosses?

### Essay Work

Write an account describing and explaining the distinctive characteristics of carboniferous limestone scenery. Use examples from the Ingleborough area if you wish and draw diagrams to illustrate your work.

### Photograph question

Identify and describe the scenes in the two photographs which were both taken from Keld Bank (747773).

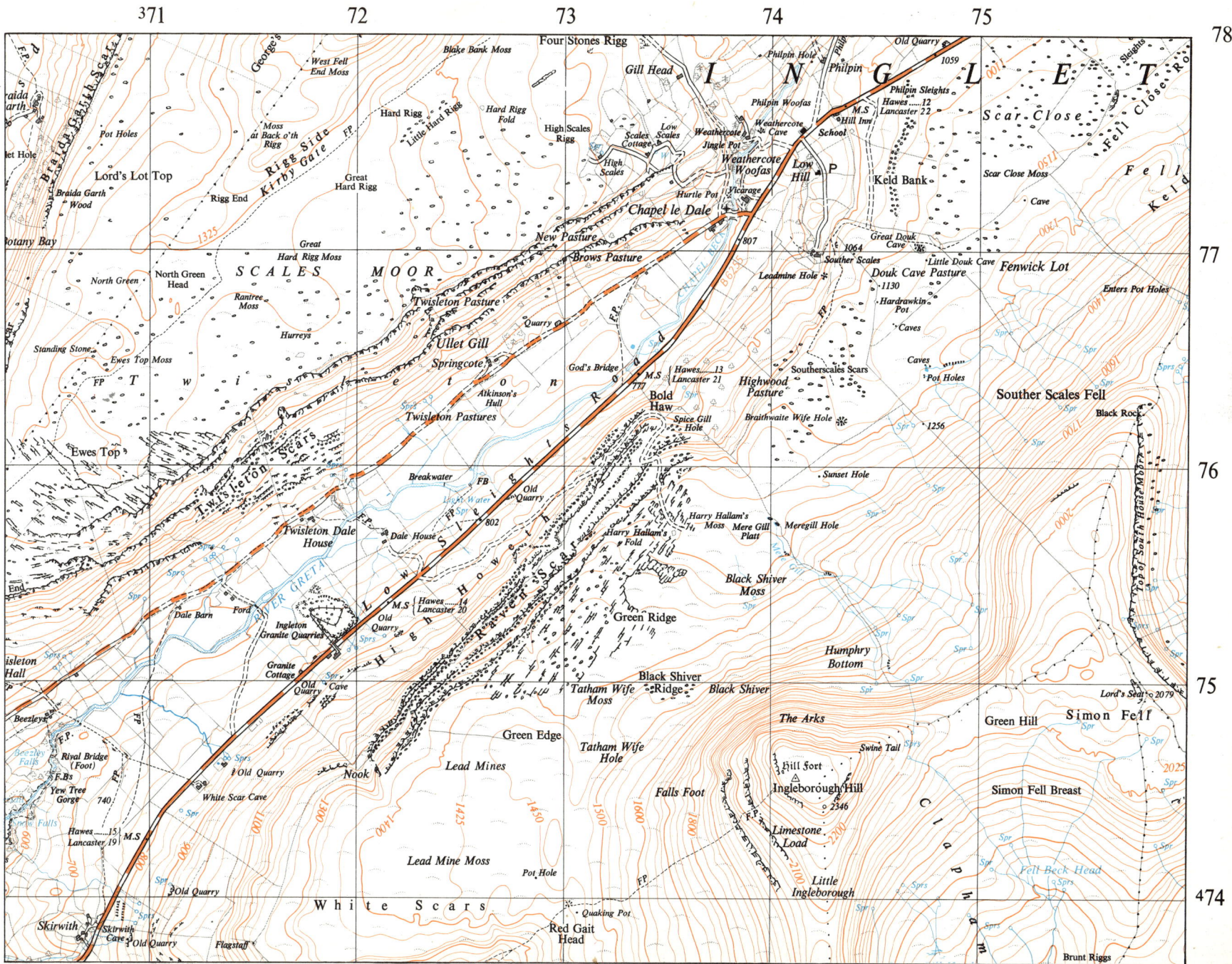

Four Stones Rigg

Blake Bank Moss

West Fell End Moss

Gill Head   I N G L E T

Philpin Hole

Philpin

Braida Garth Scar

George's

Rigg Side

Hard Rigg

Little Hard Rigg

Hard Rigg Fold

High Scales Rigg

Philpin Woofas

Philpin Sleights

Hawes .... 12
Lancaster 22

M.S

Scar-Close

Pot Holes

Moss at Back o'th Rigg

Kirby Gate

High Scales

Scales Cottage

Low Scales

Weathercote

Weathercote Cave

Hill Inn

School

Lord's Lot Top

Braida Garth Wood

Rigg End

Great Hard Rigg

Jingle Pot

Weathercote Woofas

Low Hill

P

Keld Bank

Scar Close Moss

Fell Keld

Botany Bay

1325

Great Hard Rigg Moss

Hurtle Pot

Vicarage

Chapel le Dale

1064

Souther Scales

Great Douk Cave

Cave

77     New Pasture   807   Little Douk Cave   Fenwick Lot    77

North Green Head

SCALES MOOR

Brows Pasture

Leadmine Hole

Douk Cave Pasture

1130

Hardrawkin Pot

Caves

North Green

Raniree Moss

Great Hard Rigg Moss

Twisleton Pasture

Quarry

Hurreys

Ullet Gill

Springcote

God's Bridge

Hawes .... 13
Lancaster 21

M.S

Highwood Pasture

Southerscales Scars

Caves

Pot Holes

Enters Pot Holes

Standing Stone

Ewes Top Moss

FP T w i s l e t o n

Atkinson's Hull

Twisleton Pastures

Bold Haw

777

Spice Gill Hole

1256

Souther Scales Fell

Black Rock

Ewes Top

Twisleton Scars

Breakwater

FB

Old Quarry

Braithwaite Wife Hole

Sunset Hole

76     Light Water   802   Harry Hallam's Moss   Mere Gill   Meregill Hole    76

Twisleton Dale House

Dale House

High Sleights Road

Harry Hallam's Fold

Mere Gill Platt

Black Shiver Moss

RIVER GRETA

Dale Barn

Ford

Low Sleights Road

Raven Scar

Green Ridge

Humphry Bottom

isleton Hall

Ingleton Granite Quarries

Old Quarry

Hawes .... 14
Lancaster 20

M.S

Lord's Seat 2079

Green Hill

Simon Fell

Beezleys

Granite Cottage

Old Quarry

Cave

Black Shiver Ridge

Tatham Wife Moss

Black Shiver

The Arks

Swine Tail

Simon Fell Breast

Beezley Falls

FP

Nook

Green Edge

Lead Mines

Tatham Wife Hole

Hill Fort

Ingleborough Hill

2346

Yew Tree Gorge

740

White Scar Cave

Falls Foot

Limestone Load

Hawes .... 15
Lancaster 19

M.S

Lead Mine Moss

Pot Hole

Little Ingleborough

Fell Beck Head

74     Skirwith   Skirwith Cave   Old Quarry   Flagstaff   W h i t e   S c a r s   Quaking Pot   Red Gait Head   Clapham   Brunt Riggs    474

**EXTRACT FROM 1:25 000 O.S. MAP (FIRST SERIES) SHEET SD77**

# DOWNHAM MARKET AND THE FENS

**Drainage schemes in the Fens:** The Fenland was formerly a vast marsh in which grew sedges, reeds, and similar plants. The decay of this vegetation led to the growth of a thick layer of peat. Near the Wash, the peat has been covered subsequently by marine silts. Reclamation of this marshland has been progressing for many centuries. Early schemes were small scale and sporadic; they generally extended out from the winding ridges of land which cross the fens and which provided many of the early sites for settlement. Today it is possible to distinguish on a map between the long-established, smaller, irregular drainage patterns and the more recently made long, straight cuts and drains of much larger schemes. The road patterns of the two types, that is the long-established and the more recent, are very similar to the drainage patterns.

One of the earliest large schemes was undertaken by the Dukes of Bedford in the seventeenth century when a large tract known as the Bedford Level was reclaimed. The meandering River Ouse was partly replaced by straight cuts known as the Old Bedford River and the Hundred Foot River in order to carry water more quickly to the sea. The land between these cuts was left as a wash, that is an area which could be flooded so as to hold back water and prevent flooding farther downstream.

A great step forward came with the introduction of steam pumps in place of the old wind pumps. This was in the early nineteenth century. Many of the fields are below river level and pumps are needed to lift the water from the drainage canals into the river. Today the steam pumps have been replaced by diesel and electric pumps.

The drainage systems which appear on the map extract of the Downham Market area merit special attention. In 1953 the River Ouse overflowed, breaking its banks at places between Denver and the sea. In 1956 a scheme was put into operation in which a straight channel immediately above Denver sluice was excavated; this was dug alongside the Great Ouse, joining up again with the main river very near its estuary and just above King's Lynn. The function of this channel is to ensure that flood water does not build up at the crucial Denver junction of watercourses. The Ouse, for several kilometres above Denver, has been widened to improve the flow of water from the Ely area to the Wash. Also, in 1960 a 'cut-off' channel was excavated in order to carry excess water from the upper courses of the Lark, Little Ouse, and Wissey to the new relief channel at Denver.

**Farming and settlement in the Fens:** Now the Fenland is one of the most productive farming areas in Britain. The deep, fertile soils have encouraged farmers to concentrate on intensive forms of arable farming, and about 80 per cent of the land surface is used in this way. The little permanent grassland that exists is mainly found on the washes and along the river banks. There are very few cattle and sheep. Although the farms are small, about half of them being below 25 hectares, the farmers' incomes are above the average for the country as a whole. This is because they concentrate on the production of valuable cash crops and use intensive methods of farming. Cash crops are those which are grown for sale as opposed to those which are used as fodder for livestock kept on the farm. The intensive methods used include heavy manuring and careful cultivation which give a high yield per hectare. Wheat, sugar beet, and potatoes are the most important general

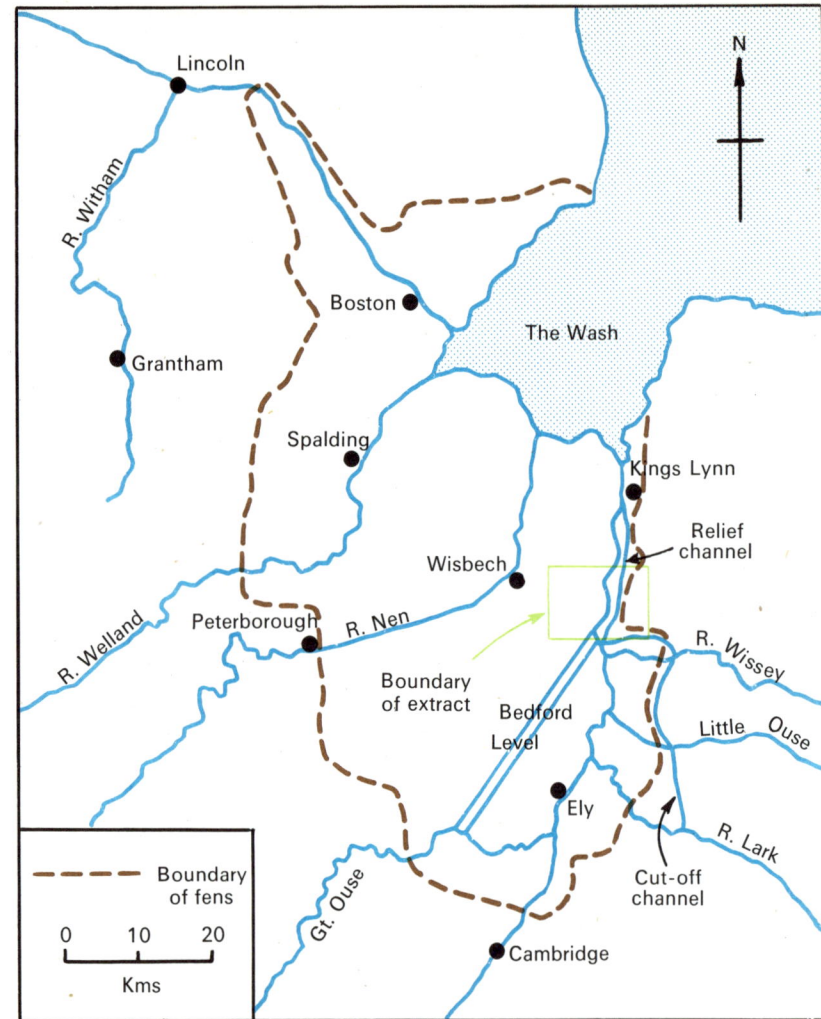

FIGURE 28
**The Fens**

farm crops, but throughout the fens there are scattered but very important pockets of market gardens and orchards.

Most of the older towns and villages are located on slightly rising ground at the edge of the Fenland or on 'islands' where gravel or clay pockets form low mounds or ridges which were built up by the old courses of rivers. However, much of the recent settlement is dispersed and straggles along roads so that often one village merges into the next.

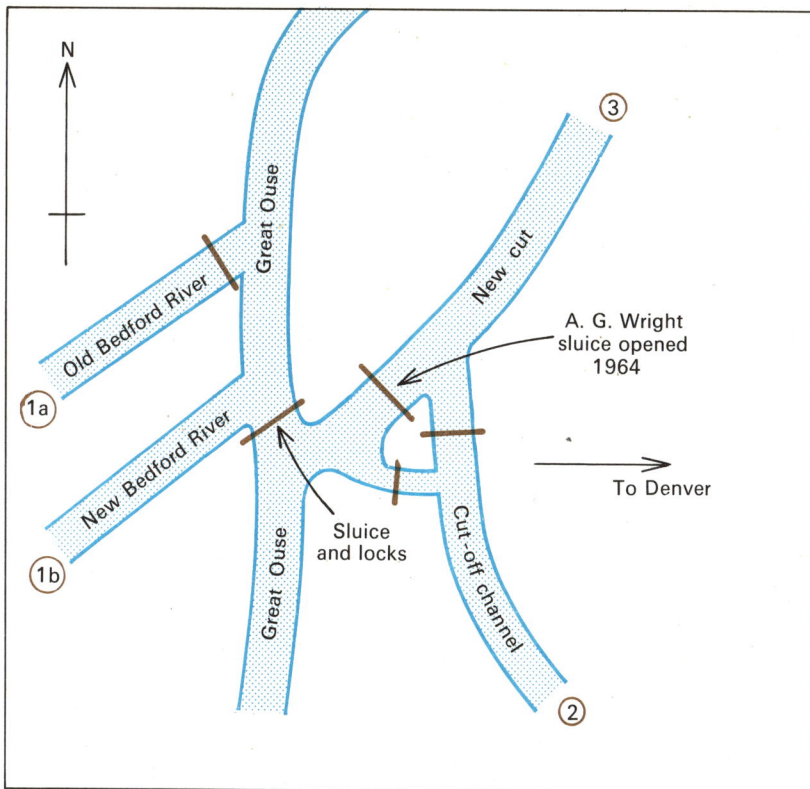

FIGURE 29
**The Denver Sluice complex**
What is the function of 1a, 1b, 2 and 3?

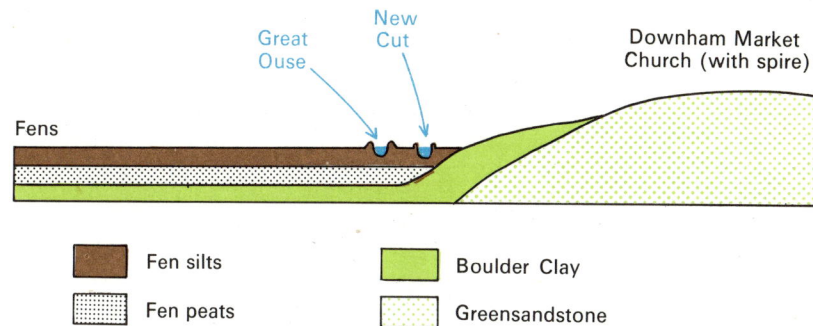

FIGURE 30
**Section across the area covered by the Downham Market extract**

garage, public house, chapel, and recreation ground. The land on Stow Bardolph Fen has no marked speciality as is found, for example, around Wisbech, where there are considerable pockets of land occupied by market gardens and orchards, or Spalding, where market gardening and bulb and greenhouse production cover considerable areas. Here on Stow Bardolph Fen general farm crops are intermingled with market garden crops and every available space is used; for example, strips of wheat no more than 15 metres wide were being grown between houses on the roadside.

Land use along the transect given as a percentage: wheat 27; barley 14; potatoes 20; sugar beet 15; onions 3; cabbages 3; lettuce 2; beans 3; beetroot 1; strawberries 6; sweet peas 1; greenhouses and their surrounds 3; pasture and waste 1; playing field 1.

*(2) Notes made on an eight-kilometre transect on land to the east of Downham Market, on the greensandstone outcrop.*

This area provided a very different scenery to that on the fen silts. Here we are back to tall hedgerows and mixed farming. The less fertile greensandstone has considerable remnants of deciduous woodland, and there are plantations both of deciduous and coniferous trees. Settlement is concentrated in a number of nucleated villages but there are a few large scattered farmhouses.

Land use along the transect given as a percentage: wheat 24; barley 8; pasture 48; woodland 20.

*Exercise :* Make two pie graphs to illustrate the two sets of statistics. Start by drawing two circles each with a radius of 4 cms, multiply each of the given percentages by 3·6 and then divide the circles into slices using the figures you have calculated. Using a protractor, each figure will be used as an angle from the centre of the circle. Shade each segment in distinctive colours, using the same colour scheme on each diagram, and label.

**Land Use Accounts:** In order to make a quick and simple appreciation of the land use of an area, a land use transect showing crops grown along a set line may be of value. It might only be possible to do this along a roadside, but such a transect may give a distorted impression. In the Fens, for example, one would expect to find a greater proportion of the most intensively cultivated crops including market garden and greenhouse production close to the farmhouse, which could be one of many alongside the road. The transect should be at least two kilometres long and one can pace the length for each crop or merely count the land use of each field. However, in the Fens this latter method is useless since the land is frequently cultivated in strips which may be only 20 metres wide and perhaps 500 metres long.

*(1) Notes made on an eight-kilometre transect on land to the north-west of Barroway Drove on the Stow Bardolph Fen – July 1973.*
In this area the community lives in a linear village strung out along the Barroway Drove for a distance of over 4 kilometres. The community has its own junior school,

*Photograph Aerofilms Ltd*

# QUESTIONS ON THE DOWNHAM MARKET MAP

### Exercise A

1. What is the general height of the land west of easting 60? To do this work out the average height of all the spot heights you can find. What is the highest point of land east of easting 60?
2. Give TWO reasons why there should be a flour mill at 603030.
3. Locate by means of grid references and name (a) a windmill, (b) a church with a tower, located west of the Great Ouse, and (c) the chapel in a village which has roads on both sides of a drainage channel.
4. What is (a) the distance apart in a straight line, and (b) along the nearest route by way of metalled roads, from Downham Market railway station to the level-crossing at 606070?
5. What does the map tell you of the meaning of the following words: Lode, Drove, Sluice, Wash, Dike?

### Photograph Question

Describe the scene looking south across Denver Sluice. Consider relief, drainage, field pattern, and land use.

### Exercise B

1. Draw a sketch map of the whole area shown on the map extract but reduce the scale to half that of the original. Mark on the map where you think the boundaries occur between fen silts, clay, and greensandstone (refer to the cross section); label each area. Also mark on the Great Ouse, main drainage channels, Downham Market, all the villages, railways, and main roads.
2. What measures have been taken to improve drainage and prevent flooding in this area?
3. Analyse the site and shape of Downham Market and account for its importance.
4. Compare the route followed by the north–south railway with that of the A10(T) between the northern and southern edges of the map. Give reasons for the differences.

### Essay Work

Draw a sketch map of the area around the Wash, marking in the principal rivers and the limit of the Fens. Mark and name FIVE important towns in or at the edge of the Fens.

Write a short essay on farming in the Fens explaining why the area is one of the most intensively cultivated arable areas in the British Isles and why there is very little livestock farming.

09 | 09

Forty Foot Br
PH
Rungay's Br
0

ST JAMES

h l a n d   F e n

08

Crabb's Abbey

Manor Fm

Ivy House Fm

Stowbridge

Neep's Br

Bodgers Fm

Crabb's Abbey Fm

07

Thorpland

Wallington Hall

Church (rems of)

MS

The Copse

Chiswick

South Runcton

Runc Botto

MS

T

5

12

21

22

Stow Bardolph

08

07

Hill Fm

Crown Fm

Barn Fm

06 | 06

West Head

Fences Fm

Old Podike Bank

2

2

3

Stow Hall Hospl

Park Fm

Inn P MS

8

35

Wimbotsham

P

Lower Fm

25

Home Fm

36

MP

Moat

Hall

05 | 05

Newbridge Fm

High Br

Common Lode

PH

Westerby Fm

S t o w   B a r d o l p h   F e n

Middle Level Main Drain

A 10 (T)

MS

Broomhill

30

04 | 04

Wash Fm

T

Barroway Drove Bank

Tile Fm

River Great Ouse

Bridge Fm

DOWNHAM MARKET

27

Sch

Hall

Bexwell

A 1122

30

MP

Moat

P

Cemy

39

Crow Hall

Stonehills Fm

Cold Fm

03 | 03

DOWNHAM WEST

Slate Fm

Downham Br

Mills

4

Wash Bank

Cemy Cross

MS

RYSTON

02 | 02

West Fm

MP

PH

MP

3

1

Salters Lode

Lock

White Hall Fm

Denver Sluice

Sluice Common

Hill Fm

Moat

19

Denver Hall

26

MS CH

Whin

Golf Cse

Ryston Hall

Home Fm

Mouse Hall Fm

Whindrove Fm

01 | 01

PH

A 1122

TOLL Inn

Nordelph

P

B 1094

3

Common

Kett's Oak

T

10

Basil Fm

Crossways Fm

D

00 | 00

Wood Ho

Birchfield Fm

ROMAN ROAD (course of)

Rookery Fm

Moat

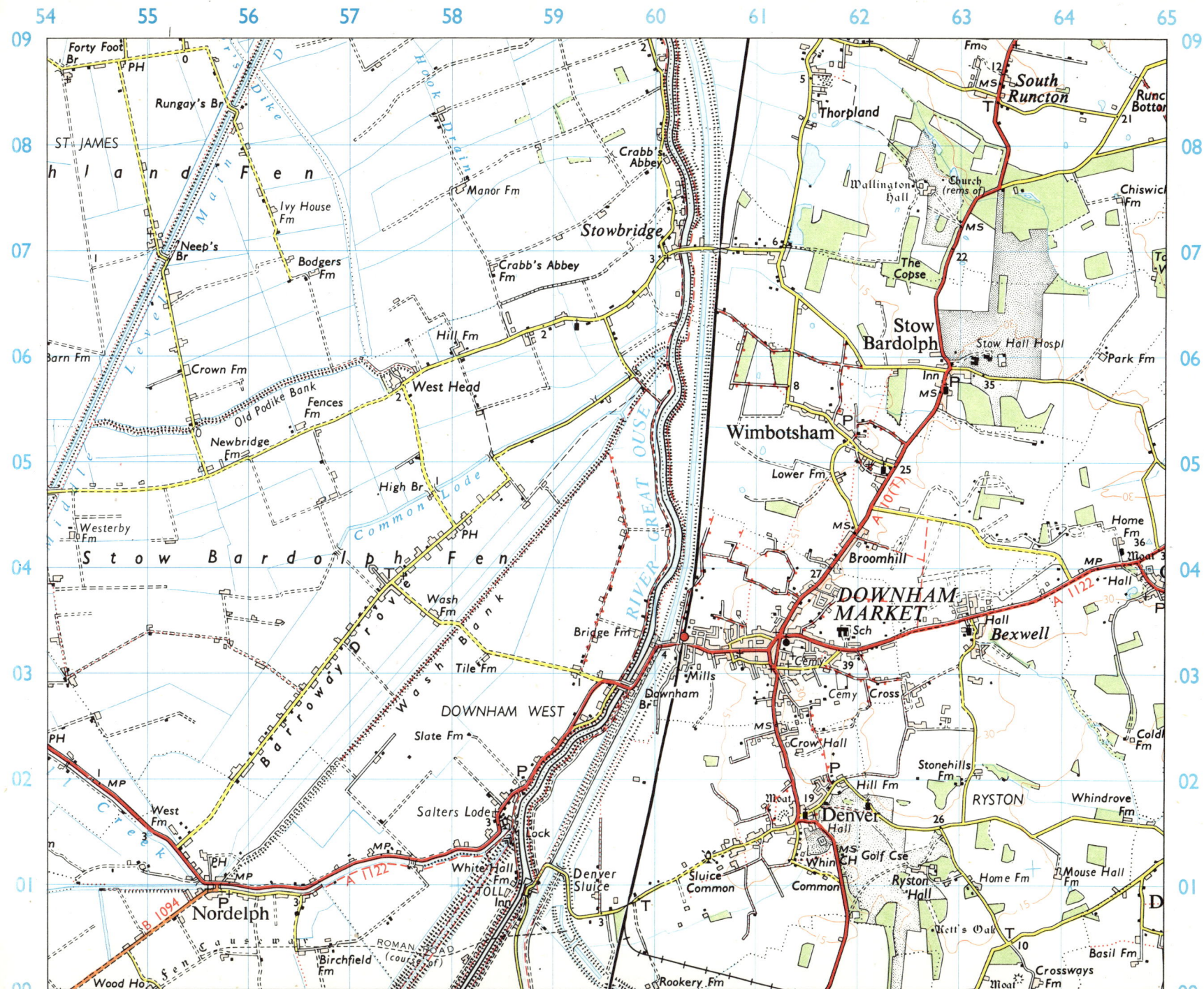

**EXTRACT FROM 1:50 000 O.S. MAP (FIRST SERIES) SHEET 143**

Reproduced from the Ordnance Survey Map with the sanction of the Controller of H.M. Stationery Office, Crown Copyright reserved.

# THE UPPER TOWY AREA OF CENTRAL WALES

**River development:** On impermeable uplands, rainwater will soon saturate the thin soils. Where there is a slope, numerous minute rivulets, perhaps a few centimetres wide, will trace intricate courses winding among the tufts of grass and heather. As these join up to form a stream of fast flowing water, a small notch is cut into the hillside, but this is not sufficient to show up on a map. In this *upland* or *moorland course*, the stream carries away small particles of soil and grains of rock. As other streams join, the supplemented watercourse is eventually sufficiently powerful to carry along small pebbles and at once its erosive power is increased enormously. This is because rock fragments carried along the floor provide the 'teeth' which wear the stream bed down. Where the bed is uneven, rock fragments may scour out pot holes which pit the beds of most mountain streams and assist in lowering them further.

A river's erosive potential is influenced by its volume, by the slope of the land and therefore the rate of flow, and the load it is carrying. However, erosion is irregular, being most marked in times of flood when boulders several tonnes in weight can be moved.

As a river cuts downwards, its banks will be subject to weathering. Soil creep down the sides of the small valley is one process; another is called freeze-thaw which occurs in winter and leads to the shattering of exposed rock faces as moisture percolates into small fissures during the day and freezes and expands at night. Thus the valley is opened up into a narrow 'v-shaped' cross section, but this shape will depend very much on the resistance of the rock. If it is very resistant, there may be precipitous faces, broken only where tributary streams join the main one. The stage in river development we have considered in this paragraph is known as that of *youth*.

The next stage is where the stream is beginning to open up a valley floor. A typical feature of the youthful stage is that of a stream winding a deeply incised course between interlocking spurs; as the stream is following this course there is a tendency for the current to be most marked on the outer and downstream sides of its bends. At these points the river bank is being cut into, and consequently the spurs of high land are being worn back until eventually the river swings from side to side across its valley floor, with alluvial flats being formed of material deposited in time of flood. When this stage has been reached we can say the river has reached a *stage of maturity*, or is in its *valley stage*.

Theoretically then we have considered that a river passes through an upland or moorland stage, then a youthful stage, and then a valley or mature stage. Figure 31 illustrates these but if you study the courses of many of the rivers shown on the Upper Towy extract you will notice very similar features.

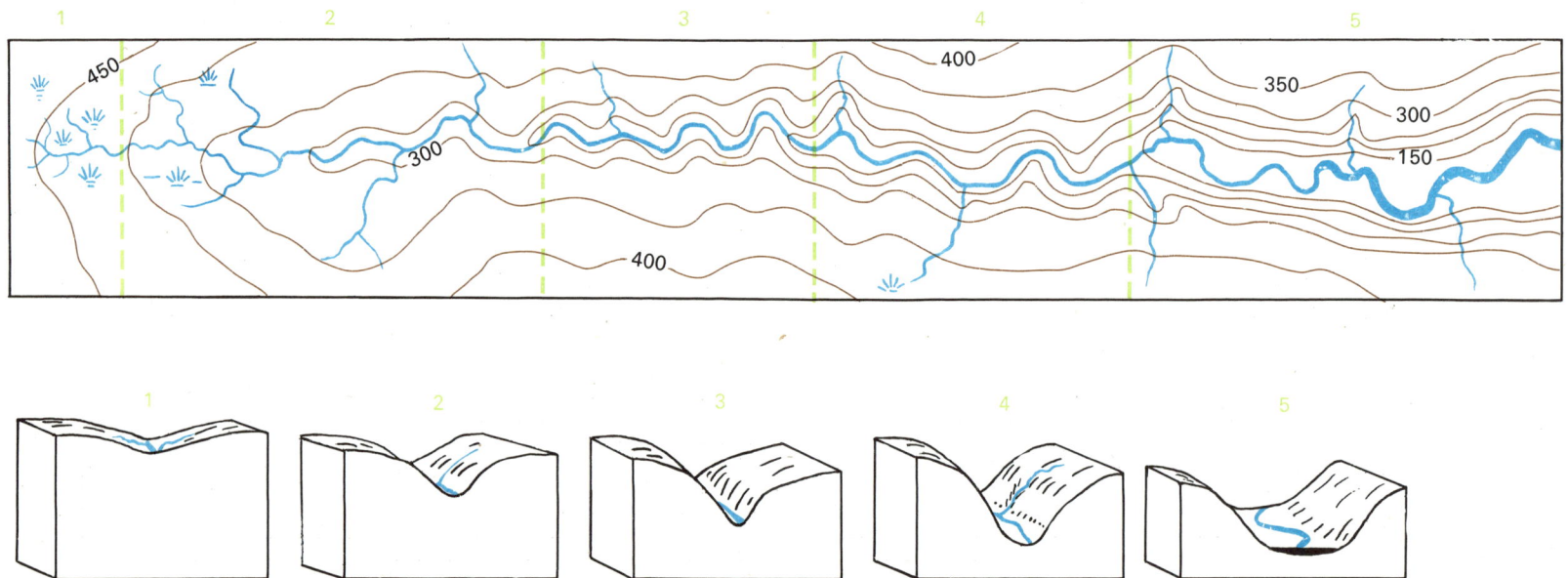

FIGURE 31
**River development in Central Wales**

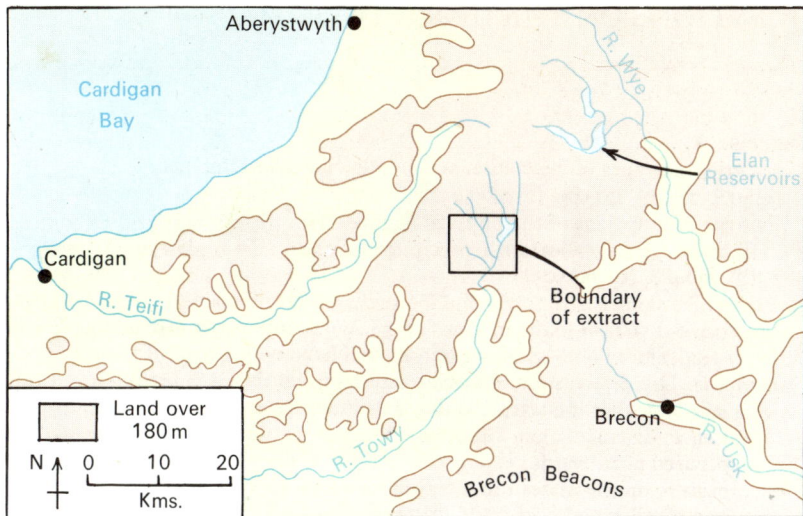

FIGURE 32
**Central Wales**

**The Upper Towy Extract:** First locate the extract by studying figure 32. A section drawn across the extract would show that the upper surfaces between the valleys have a remarkably even level; in places these interfluves are narrow plateaux and in places they are more rounded, but in either case they rise to a height of just over 400 metres. This feature is apparent in much of Central Wales, where the ancient rocks of Ordovician and Silurian age have been worn down to a peneplain and then re-elevated. Three such surfaces of peneplanation can be recognised as shown in figure 33. This extract is taken from a portion of the middle plateau which

has been eaten into to form a greatly dissected landscape. The rock is impermeable, much of it being a slaty mudstone, and the rainfall is over 1800mm per annum so that processes of river erosion are very active. On the uplands where the land is level or slightly sloping, there are extensive peat bogs which reach a great depth locally where poorly drained hollows occur.

However, the present relief is not solely the result of river erosion on an uplifted plateau of ancient hard rock. There are traces of glacial deposits in some of the valleys, and although these do not have the spectacular glacial features found in mountainous areas such as Helvellyn, nevertheless there is no doubt that the main valleys on the extract have been deepened by glacial action.

**Forestry:** In recent years the Forestry Commission has added considerable tracts of this area to its afforestation schemes. The Sitka spruce responds better than most conifers to the ill-drained, very acid, marshy tracts on the plateaux above 350 metres, although some pine is found at these levels also. On the valley sides however a much wider range of species will tolerate the more sheltered, better drained terrain.

**Reservoirs:** Consider the following factors:
(1) Heavy rainfall. *What is the annual rainfall in this area?*
(2) Deep gorges. *Calculate how deep and how wide the most well-developed gorges are on this extract.*
(3) Impermeable rocks which have experienced little shattering. *What age and what type of rock is found here and what has shattering got to do with this topic?*
(4) Isolated, with a low density of population. *Estimate the density of population for this extract. What is the area of each grid square on the extract? Is the average density over 25, 10 to 25, 1 to 10 or under 1?*
(5) Increasing demands for water. *What is the nearest industrial region to this area?*

With these factors in mind it is not surprising that more reservoirs are being established in Central Wales. The River Towy Scheme for the West Glamorgan Water Board was officially opened in 1973; it involved the construction of Brianne Dam behind which are impounded the waters of the upper Towy to form Llyn Brianne.

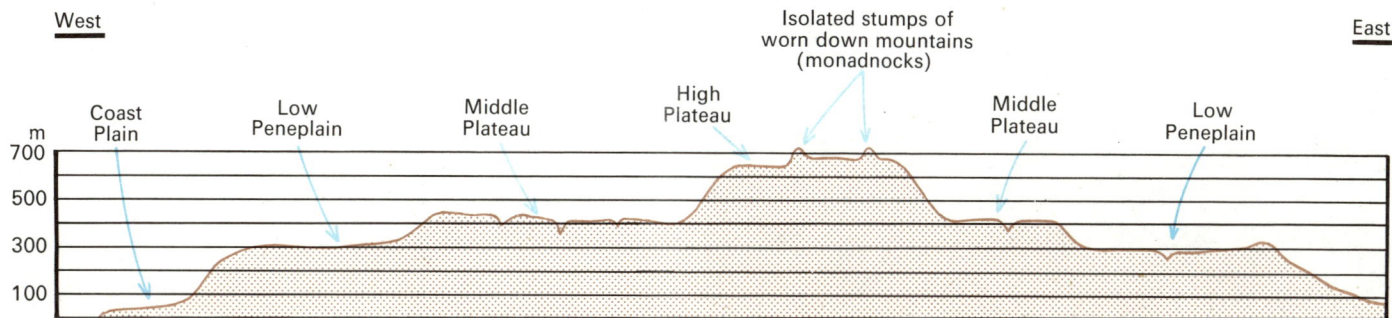

FIGURE 33
**Relief section across Central Wales**

33

# QUESTIONS ON THE UPPER TOWY MAP

## Exercise A

1. Identify the types of vegetation at the following grid references:
   (a) 724522, (b) 721509, (c) 785505.
2. Pair the descriptions of the physical features with the relevant grid references:
   (i) a col, (ii) a valley with precipitous slopes, (iii) a plateau; (a) 718465, (b) 779488, (c) 755505.
3. Plan a hike along roads, tracks and footpaths which are marked on the map from the bridge at 764451 to the road at 717538. Work out precise instructions for the party leader to follow assuming that he will have both a map of the area and a compass. Divide the route you give into legs and for each leg point out how long it is and what the terrain is like. For example:

   Leg 2; distance 3 km. Climb up from the west of the building at 763484; proceed northwards keeping the scar face to your left. Continue over rough pasture on the plateau top, travelling north westwards for 2 km. Descend into a valley and pass building 744509 on your immediate right.

## Practical Work

Enlarge an area of the map between eastings 75 and 78 and north of northing 50. Draw in contour lines and drainage courses and build this up into a three-dimensional model. A minimum workable size for the model is probably 15 cms by 20 cms.

## Exercise B

1. Draw a sketch section from 730480 to 760500. Mark where the two watercourses cross the line of the section. In what ways do the two valleys differ?
2. Describe the relief and drainage of the area south of northing 47.
3. Relate the settlement and communications to the physical geography of the area.
4. Study the photographs on this page and then describe the cross section of the valley in each of the scenes. Locate a similar cross section of a valley for each of the illustrations on the map extract and give the relevant six-figure reference. Then describe the stage in the development of the valley at each of the three points.

## Essay Work

What factors must engineers consider when choosing a site for a reservoir and what problems, both physical and human, can they meet? How might these be overcome?

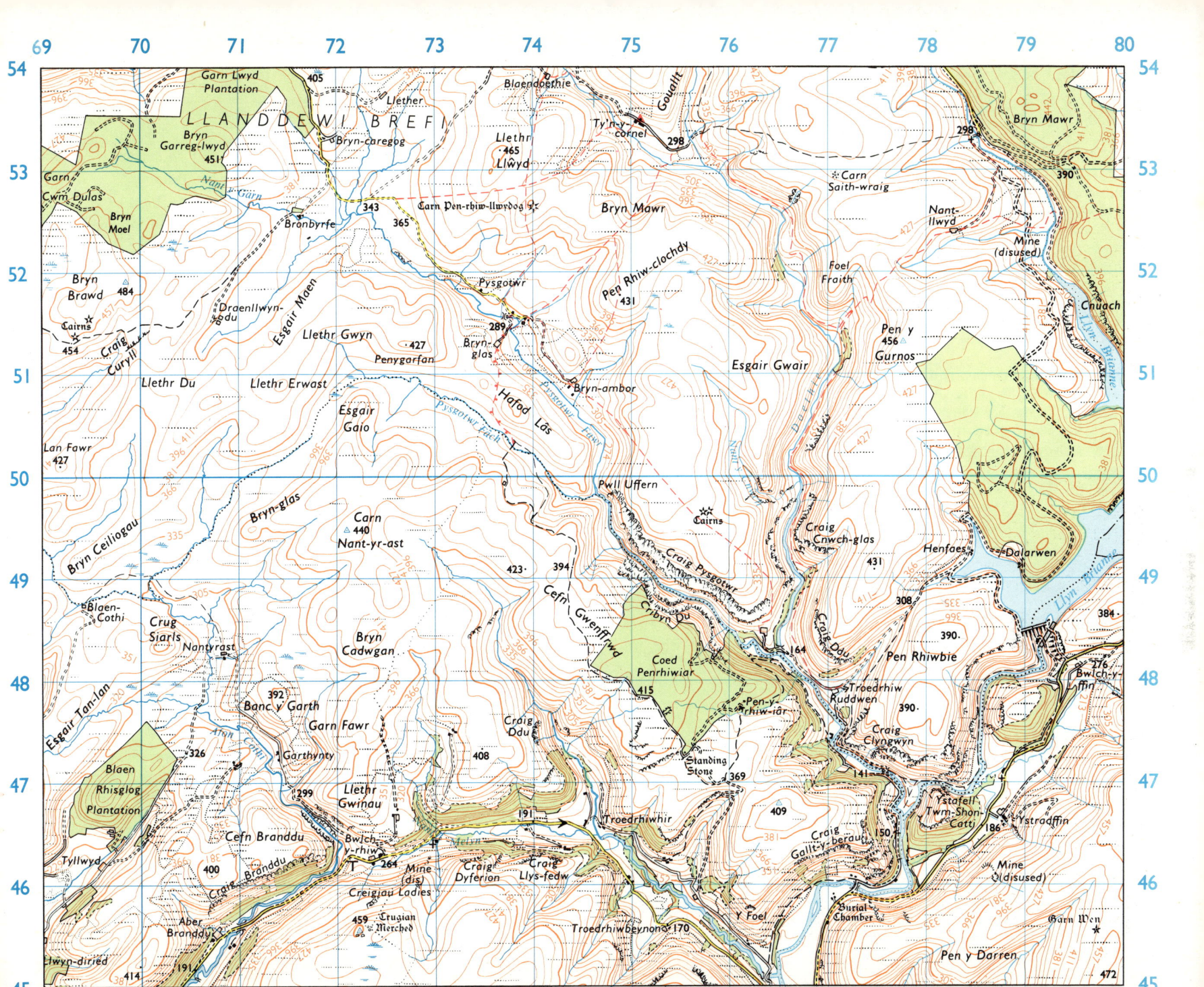

35

# MILFORD HAVEN

For many years Britain was dependent upon coal to satisfy most of its energy requirements. However, the discovery of new sources of energy (oil, natural gas, and atomic energy) meant that, although coal was still important particularly in the generation of electricity, it no longer contributed such a high percentage to our total energy demands. Whilst resources are available, petroleum is expected to be the most important source of energy. As yet Britain produces little petroleum itself, relying on imports mainly from countries surrounding the Persian Gulf. Petroleum is cheaper to transport in the crude state, hence the development of refineries along our coastline in places where there are facilities to accommodate the enormous tankers now in service. One area capable of receiving these tankers is Milford Haven.

**Milford Haven:** If you study the map on page 38 you will see that Milford Haven is the name given both to the estuary of the River Cleddau and the main town on its north bank. The estuary was at one time a river valley carved out of the underlying Old Red Sandstone and then submerged as the sea level rose. We call this feature a ria, and there are other examples to be found in south Devon and Cornwall.

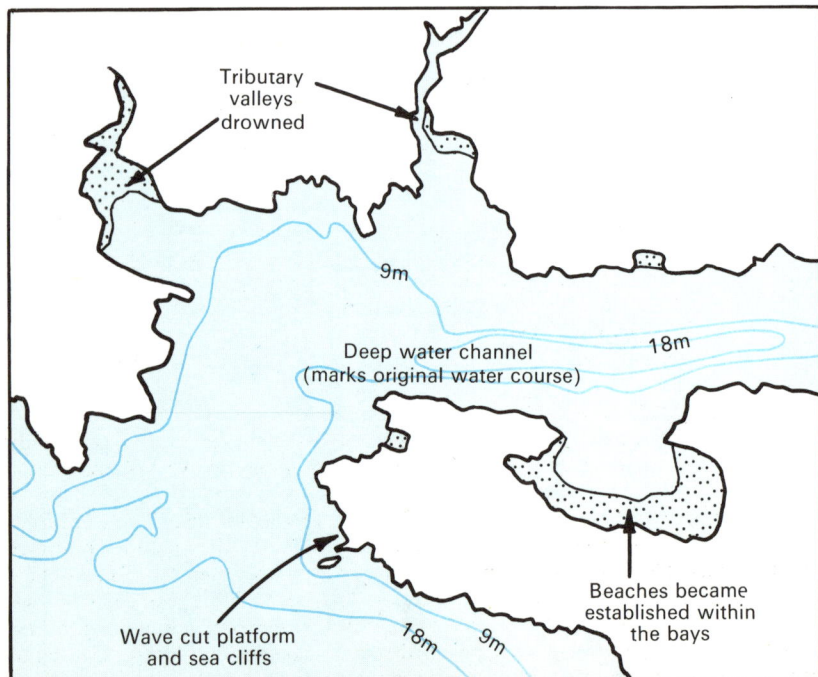

FIGURE 34
**Milford Haven ria**

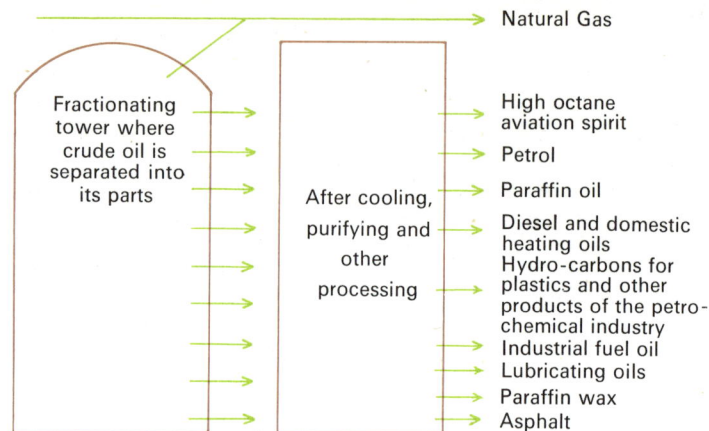

FIGURE 35
**The fractionating tower**

**The Refineries at Milford Haven:** The most important factor determining the siting of this refinery complex is deep water. This has attracted Esso, B.P., Gulf, Texaco, and Amoco to establish refineries there. Further dredging has allowed tankers of 270 000 tonnes access to the unloading berths. With this facility, with the availability of land for building, and with a situation suited to tankers coming from the Middle East, Milford Haven now handles over 40 million tonnes of crude oil each year.

Crude oil is of little use in an unrefined state. The function of the refinery is to separate out the different products that we have come to regard as essential to our way of life – petrol, lubricating oils, and diesel fuel. This it does in a fractionating tower where the crude oil is boiled. The lightest materials are removed at the top of the tower, with the heavier fractions being drawn off as liquid side streams.

A small percentage of the refined oil from Milford Haven travels by road and rail. The majority is re-exported in smaller tankers for distribution around our coasts, or piped directly to the Midlands and North-West of England. Some is retained for use in nearby electricity generating stations and an expanding petro-chemical manufacturing complex.

**The conflict between industrial development and conservation:** The refineries at Milford Haven straddle the boundary of the Pembrokeshire National Park. Although employment is assured for some 2000 workers, keen conservationists are apprehensive as to the effect these refineries will have upon this area of outstanding natural beauty. The oil companies themselves have spent a large amount of money in reshaping the land so that the refineries are hidden from view. In combating pollution they have applied noise controls to machinery, run effluent through oil filters to ensure the purity of the estuary, and built tall chimneys to release combustible gases high into the air.

*Exercise:* Make a list of all the National Parks in Britain. Does a conflict between industry and conservation occur in any of the areas you have listed? Under what conditions should industry be allowed in areas designated as places of natural beauty?

# HIGH MARNHAM

**The Trent Vale:** From Burton-on-Trent in Staffordshire to the Humber, the River Trent takes a meandering course within a flood plain which is generally not much wider than three kilometres. The gradient of the river throughout this stretch of its course is very gentle so that it is unable to continue deepening its channel any further. Instead it winds its way from side to side across the flood plain, occasionally impinging against solid rocks and there forming steep river cliffs known as bluffs. The meander loops may become more accentuated in time until eventually the meander is cut off and the course of the river straightened. Portions of the abandoned course of the river can often be detected on a map; sometimes for example a parish or county boundary follows the abandoned course of the river rather than the present one.

Settlement established before the present century was usually absent from the flood plain, but a line of villages on either side have been established on the firm foundations of terraces. These terraces may well represent a former, wider flood plain of the Trent which has subsequently been rejuvenated, enabling it to erode its present flood plain. Nowadays embankments afford protection from flooding, and the flat valley floor can be settled on. The river is navigable downstream from Nottingham for barges of up to 200 tonnes and the main cargoes carried include petroleum, grain, timber, gravel, cement, and coal.

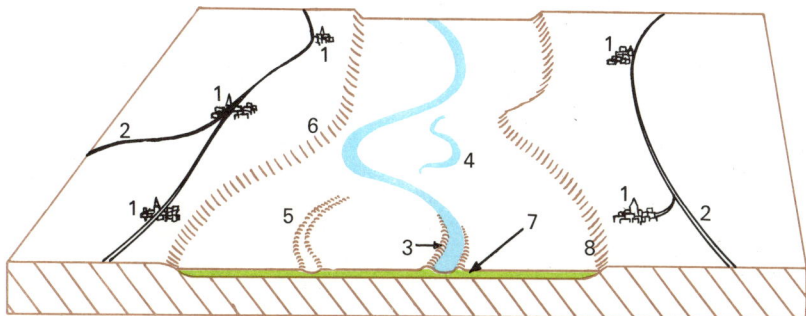

FIGURE 37

**The Trent Power Complex**

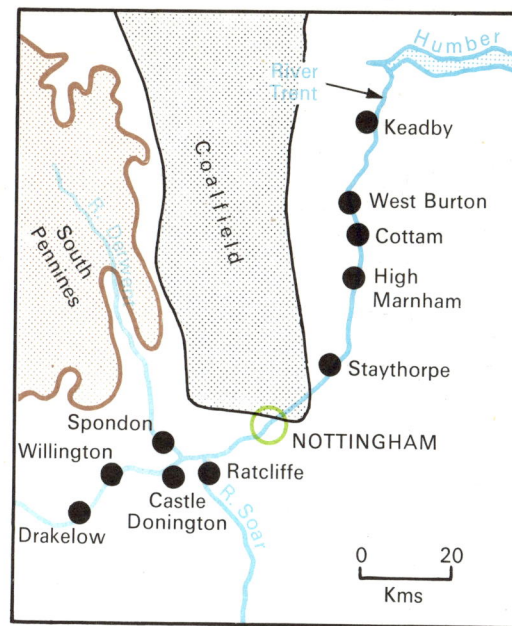

FIGURE 36

**The Trent Flood Plain below Newark**

*Exercise:* (a) Comment on the siting of the villages (1) and the courses of the roads (2).

(b) Identify: river bluff; embankment; abandoned course of river; partially abandoned course, terraces, and alluvium. These are numbered 3 to 8, but not in that order.

**Power Stations:** Electricity can be produced by using many sources including water power, atomic energy, coal, and oil. In this country by far the most important is coal. Similarly, the electric power stations provide the Coal Board with its biggest market. The largest single concentration of generating capacity in Britain lies along the banks of the River Trent. All these stations, located in figure 37, are of the conventional thermal type, using coal as the fuel. With cooling towers rising to over 100 metres and chimneys approaching 200 metres high, their physical impact is enormous. In terms of output these stations together produce approximately 20 per cent of England's electricity, much of which is transmitted to the south-east of the country. The idea of a power station catering for local demand is outdated. These power stations were located in the Trent Valley because:

(1) It is centrally situated in relation to other parts of the country.
(2) There is flat land available for construction.
(3) The fuel is easily obtainable from the nearby largest and most modernised coalfield in Britain.
(4) Water from the river can be used for the cooling process.
(5) There are facilities for the disposal of the ash from the boilers; these include its usage in the reclamation of gravel pits and the building up of low-lying land.

**High Marnham:** When it was opened in 1962, High Marnham Power Station was Britain's first one million kilowatt power station. At full load, 10 000 tonnes of East Midland's coal is used each day. This is pulverised, then carried by hot air to the boilers where it heats the purified water. The steam, superheated and at high pressure, is able to drive the turbines which control the generators that will produce electricity. The steam meanwhile passes through a condenser. The water used to cool the steam becomes warm itself and is taken to the cooling towers and then returned to the condenser. Over 120 million litres of water are required every hour for cooling, although much of this can be used again and again. The energy produced at High Marnham is fed into the country's super grid.

Winterton

B 4327

Bridge

Mullock

Butterhill

Philbeach Fm

Mabesgate

Standing Stone

Motte

Bicton

Herbrandston

Barleymoor

Studdo

Fort

Thornton

St Botolphs

Crabhall Fm

Slatehill Fm

Trewarren

St Ishmael's

Sch

PH

Sandy Haven

Hall

P

Neeston

Lodge Fm

Long Stone

HUBBERSTON

Liddeston

HAKIN

Hubberston

PH

Priory

Fort

Dalehill

Musselwick

Watch House Point

Lindsway Bay

Little Castle Head

Longoar Bay

Fort

Fort

Kilroom

Works

Gelliswick

CH

Hakin

MILFORD HAVEN

Townsend

Castle

Dale

PH

P

Dale Roads

Monk Haven

Great Castle Head

South Hook Point

Gelliswick Bay

Point Fm

Dale Fort Field Centre

Broomhill Fm

Dale Point

Maryborough Fm

Castlebeach Bay

MILFORD HAVEN

Stack Rock

HERBRANDSTON (det)

Jetty

Kete

Brunt Fm

Watwick Bay

Pembrokeshire Coast Path

Jetty

Popton Point

Jet

West Blockhouse Point

Thorn Island

ANGLE (det)

Chapel Bay

West Angle Bay

West Pill

North Hill

Lifeboat Sta

Angle Point

Sawdern Point

Bullwell

Earthwork

Sawdern

Mill Bay

Coastguard Station

CG Lookout

ST ANN'S HEAD

Rat Island

WT Sta

Danger Area

North Studdock

Angle

P

PH

Hall

Angle Bay

Eastington

Rhos

Castles Bay

South Studdock

Fort

B 4320

Hardingshill

Middlehill

Pembrokeshire Coast Path

Sheep Island

Parsonsquarry Bay

Pembrokeshire Coast Path

Jeffersonwalls

Neath

Guttle Hole

West Pickard Bay

East Pickard Bay

Black Cave

Pembrokeshire Coast Path undefined

Devil's Quoit

Mon Burial Chamber

Kilpaison Burrows

Newton

Gravel Bay

# QUESTIONS ON THE HIGH MARNHAM AND MILFORD HAVEN MAPS

## Exercise A

1. Comment on the position of (a) a lighthouse at 807028 and (b) a jetty in square 8704 (MH).
2. What direction is the triangulation pillar (823071) from Angle Church (866029) (MH)?
3. Give one piece of evidence to suggest that the River Trent is navigable (HM).
4. The following statements may be true or false. Study the map extract of High Marnham to find out:
   (a) Low Marnham (807695) is a good example of a linear-shaped village.
   (b) There is still some marshland remaining on the flood plain of the Trent.
   (c) There are many roads crossing the Trent.
   (d) There is no woodland in this area.
5. Give THREE pieces of evidence of prehistoric settlement on the Milford Haven map.

## Practical Work

Draw a map on the same scale as the High Marnham extract. Mark on it the Trent and its tributaries; draw and label the course of the A1133, and mark and label the position of the main settlements.

Comment on the sites and positions of these settlements.

## Exercise B

1. Describe and account for the distribution of industry on the Milford Haven extract.
2. Compare the coastal features from Sheep Island (843017) to Gravel Bay (878006) with those from Dale Point (825052) to Monk Haven (828064) (MH).
3. Explain why there is little settlement south of the B4320 (MH).
4. Describe the course of the River Trent and the form of its flood plain.

## Essay Work

Give as many examples as you can of recent industrial development which is to some degree dependent upon a site close to water. Describe and illustrate with sketch maps the various examples you use.

**left:** EXTRACT FROM 1:50 000 O.S. MAP (FIRST SERIES) SHEET 157
**right:** EXTRACT FROM 1:50 000 O.S. MAP (FIRST SERIES) SHEET 121

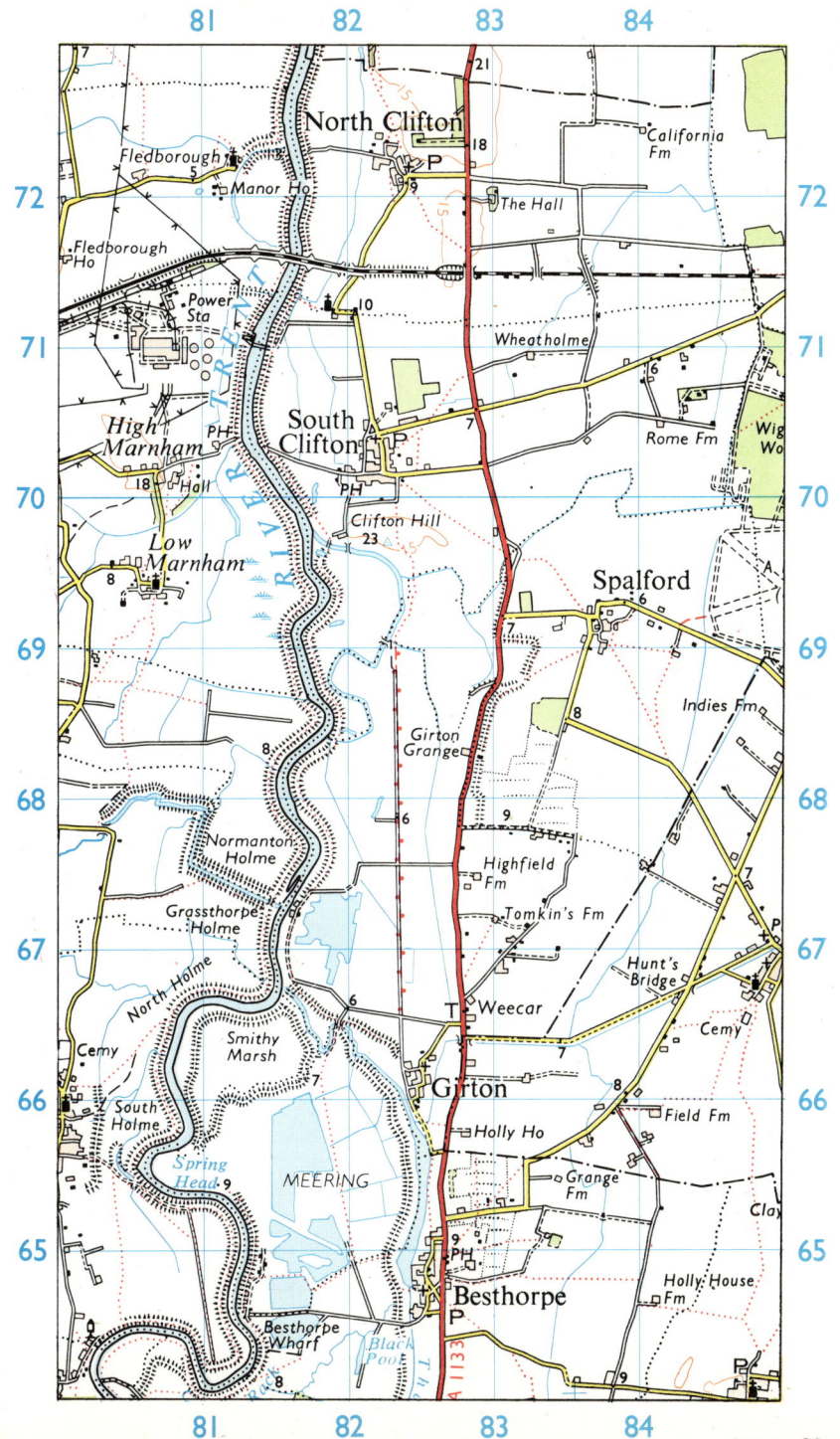

# HELVELLYN

During the Ice Age, glaciers and ice sheets covered much of the British Isles as far south as the Thames valley and lower Severn. Large areas of the lowlands were influenced by glacial deposition including boulder clay, sands and gravels left by the ice sheets. It is in the mountain regions, however, that we find the most striking evidence of glaciation, especially in the Highlands of Scotland, Snowdonia and the Lake District. Many features of upland glaciation are particularly well illustrated in the Helvellyn area.

Helvellyn is one of the well-known peaks in the Lake District. The rocks making up the area covered by the map extract belong to the Borrowdale Volcanic series, and are a consolidated mass of varied lavas and ashes which have been eroded to give very rugged scenery. The contour patterns on the map extract probably appear very confusing at first sight. In a case such as this you should first locate the highest stretches of land, then find where the lowest areas of land are, and finally work out which are spurs projecting from the highland and which are the valleys going up into the highland, watercourses being the obvious clue in the latter case.

Glaciation has been the major influence on the details of relief. During the Ice Age, an ice cap covered much of the Lake District although its limits must have fluctuated considerably. Tongues of ice, known as glaciers, moved outwards from the centre following the courses of the main river valleys. The ice plucked away fragments of rock and this debris then became embedded in it providing the glacier with 'teeth' to further erode its valley; this last process is known as abrasion. Thus the valleys were deepened and straightened. The lower slopes of the western portion of the Helvellyn mass form the side of such a glaciated valley. Large ribbon lakes occupy hollows in the main valleys. These hollows were scooped out by glacial erosion, and sometimes their lower ends were blocked by glacial deposits. Thirlmere is an example of such a lake. It has supplied water to Manchester since 1894. The water level of the lake has been raised artificially and the outflow controlled. Coniferous plantations have been established on its banks in order to conserve the slopes from excessive erosion and so prevent silting up.

In the later stages of the Ice Age, when much of the ice cap had decayed, snow still accumulated, often in hollows high up on the mountain sides. During the day some of the snow round the edges of such hollows may have melted and the water penetrated cracks in the rock. Freezing of this water at night could cause rock shattering. Also, as snow accumulated, the under layers would be pressurized to form ice which, in turn, would pluck away rock fragments. These processes deepened the hollows to form cirques (also known as corries and cwms). These are semi-circular basins often with an almost vertical face behind them. The ice may have finished at the lip of the cirque where a small terminal moraine would then form. Behind this today a circular lake or tarn often occupies the floor of the hollow. When two cirques eat back towards one another, the intervening upland can be worn into a sharp-edged ridge called an arete; Striding Edge is a fine example of this.

a
River valley
with tributary

b
Rock debris
Glacier occupies the valley

c
Glaciated valley
with hanging valley

FIGURE 38
**Glaciation of a river valley**

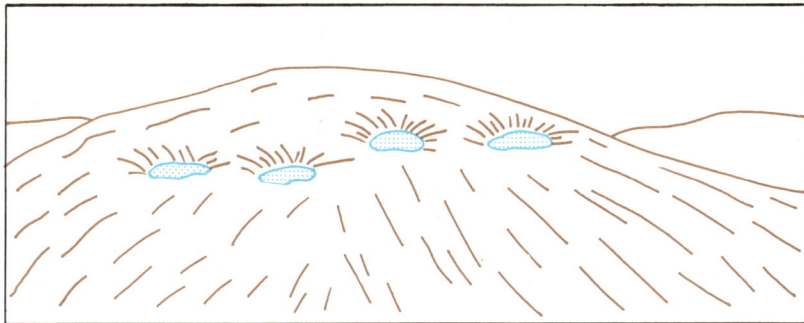

(1) Hollows with accumulating snow and ice

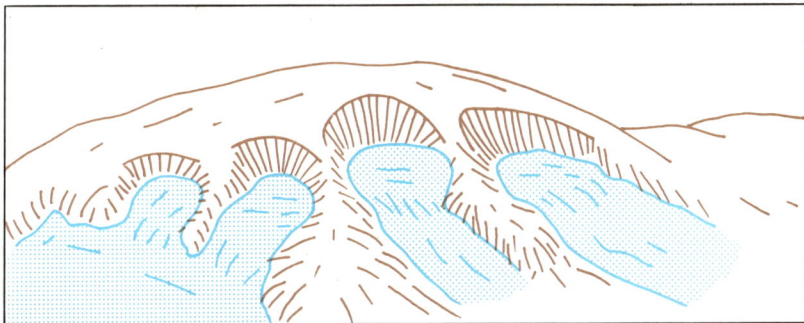

(2) Hollows being deepened: tongues of ice leading from the hollows

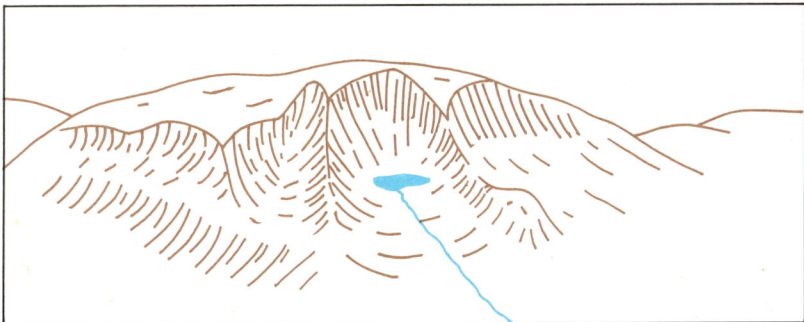

(3) After glacial action: hollows or cirques separated by razor sharp edges known as arêtes

FIGURE 39
**Development of a glaciated landscape**

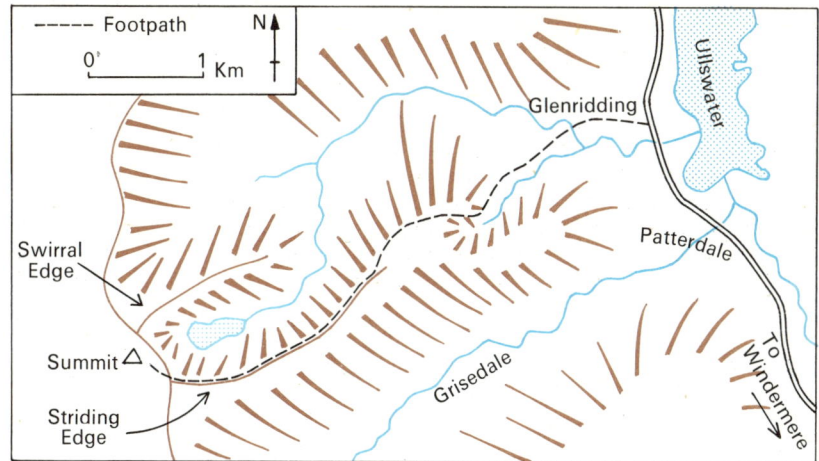

FIGURE 40
**The course of a footpath to Helvellyn summit**

**Fell Walking:** The best way to appreciate the scenery of the Lake District is on foot. For beginners to fell walking, it is as well to bear in mind a number of safeguards. First plan your route on an Ordnance Survey map. Where it is available, the 1:25 000 sheet should be used. Eight to ten kilometres, as measured on a map, is quite enough for a day's walk over rough ground if you are unused to these conditions. Keep to well-used paths and carry a pocket compass. The latter should enable you to find the correct route, if in doubt. Some walkers make a note of the bearing along which they are travelling, so that if mist obscures landmarks they can work out a back bearing and return to the point of departure. If mist does thicken, turn back immediately. Travel in parties of at least three so that, in case of accident, one can remain with the injured person whilst the third goes for help. Clothing should include stout walking boots with rubber soles, thick socks, tough trousers, sweater and a rain-proofed outer garment.

The sketch map indicates the course of a very popular walk; the return journey should take at least five hours. It is a spectacular walk and should be attempted only if you are accompanied by an experienced fell walker.

# QUESTIONS ON THE HELVELLYN MAP

**Exercise A**

1. What is the character of the land surface at 350160 and 354159?
2. Calculate the height of Red Tarn and Thirlmere above sea level.
3. Give directions to a walker who wishes to climb Helvellyn from the main road, keeping to marked footpaths. He has a compass but no map.
4. Give an example and explain what is meant by each of the following terms: Pike; Crag; Gill; Beck.

**Practical Work**

On a grid showing all the eastings and northings, mark in the 1000, 1500, 2000, 2500 and 3000 feet contours. Colour the layers green (the lowest land), yellow, orange, light brown, dark brown and black respectively. Print the words CIRQUE, ARETE, TARN and SUMMIT in the correct places.

If you wish, you can make a layer model using the map you have made.

**Exercise B**

1. Draw a sketch section along a line from 340170 to 350140; mark and name on it any features which you associate with glaciation. Explain the origin of these features.
2. Study the course and valley of Nethermostcove Beck from its source to its junction with Grisedale Beck. Describe and give reasons for the shape of its valley at 346147, 348144, 353143 and 358144.
3. Why does the lake shore protrude slightly at 323137?
4. Comment on the distribution of woodland.

**Essay Work**

Why is the Lake District such a popular tourist centre?

**Photograph Question**

Make sketches of the scenes shown in the photographs and then, using information given on the map extract, label as many features as possible.

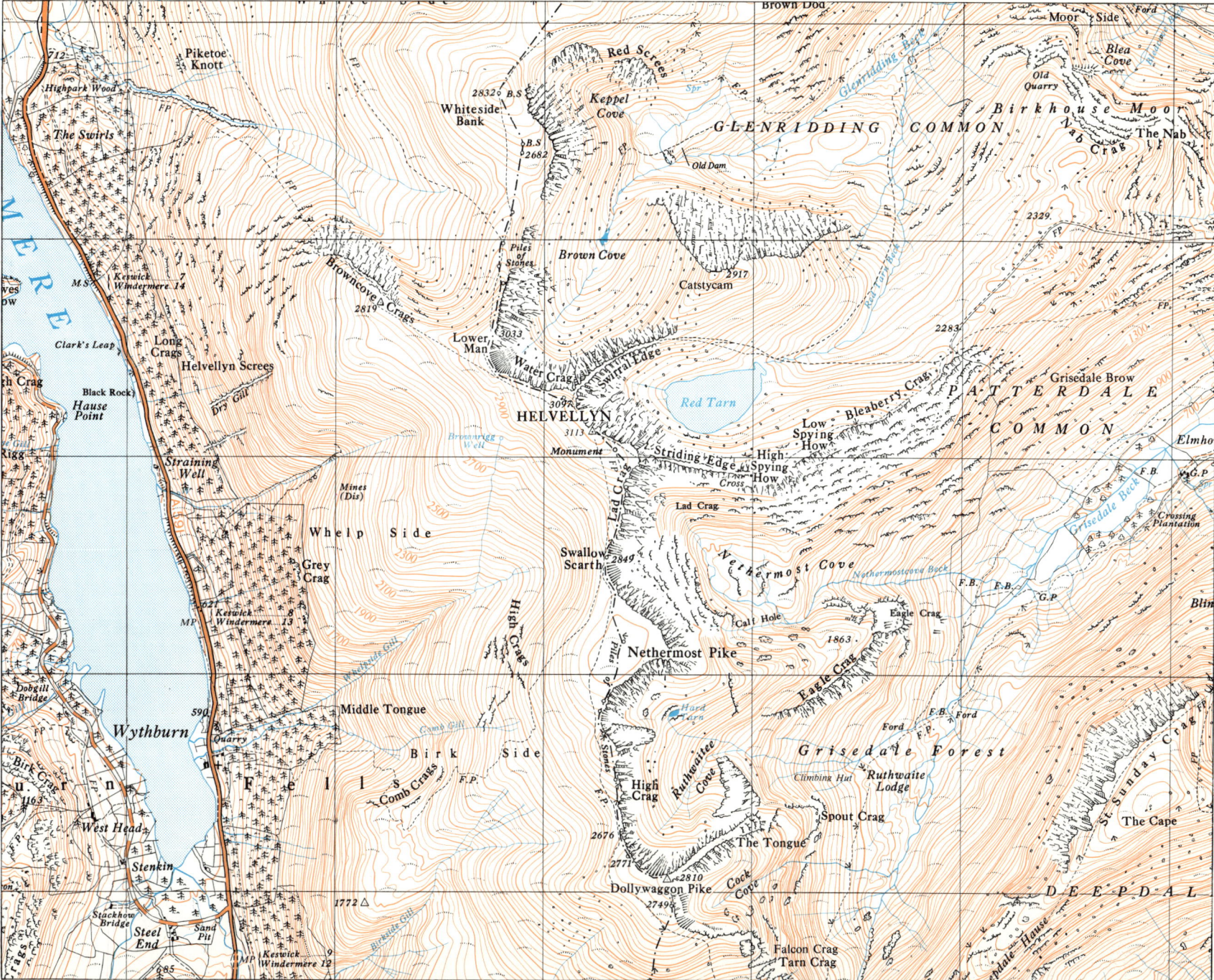

Piketoe Knott
Highpark Wood
712
The Swirls
MERE
M.S.
Keswick Windermere 14
Clark's Leap
Long Crags
Helvellyn Screes
Dry Gill
Black Rock
Hause Point
Straining Well
Whelp Side
Grey Crag
621
Keswick Windermere 13
MP
Browncove Crags
2819
Lower Man
3033
Water Crag
3097
HELVELLYN
3113
Monument
Brunriggg Well
Mines (Dis)
High Crags
Middle Tongue
590
Quarry
Wythburn
Birk Crag
u. 1163
West Head
Stenkin
Dobgill Bridge
Birkside Gill
Comb Crags
Birk Side
Dunmail Gill
FELLS
Stackhow Bridge
Steel End
Sand Pit
685
Keswick Windermere 12

Brown Dod
Red Screes
Keppel Cove
Whiteside Bank
2832 B.S
B.S 2682
Old Dam
GLENRIDDING COMMON
Brown Cove
Catstycam
2917
Piles of Stones
Swirral Edge
Red Tarn
Striding Edge
Cross
Lad Crag
Lad Crag
Swallow Scarth
2849
Nethermost Cove
Nethermostcove Beck
Calf Hole
Nethermost Pike
1863
Hard Tarn
Stones
Ruthwaitee Cove
Eagle Crag
High Crag
2676
Climbing Hut
Ruthwaite Lodge
Spout Crag
The Tongue
2771
Dollywaggon Pike
2810
2749
Cock Cove
Falcon Crag
Tarn Crag
1772

Moor Side
Ford
Blea Cove
Old Quarry
Birkhouse Moor
Nab Crag
The Nab
2329
Low Spying How
Bleaberry Crag
High Spying How
PATTERDALE
COMMON
Grisedale Brow
Elmho
2283
F.B.
G.P
Grisedale Beck
Crossing Plantation
F.B.
G.P
Blin
Eagle Crag
Ford
Eagle Crag
F.B. Ford
Grisedale Forest
Ford F.P
St. Sunday Crag
The Cape
DEEPDAL
Grisedale Hause

A591

332   33   34   35   36   337
517
16
15
14
513

**EXTRACT FROM 1:25 000 O.S. MAP (FIRST SERIES) SHEET NY31**

43

**The South Wales Region:** South Wales is sometimes recognised merely as a coal-mining area. Although its industrial development has in the past been based on coal, even this is not true today. Much of South Wales has not been industrialised at all. The fertile coastal lowland composed of marls, sandstone and limestone (known as the Vale of Glamorgan) still retains much of its rural character. In the north of the Vale this situation is changing as the presence of the main lines of communication between Swansea and Cardiff have encouraged industrial development. This growth has been further stimulated by the movement of people from the coalfield as the industries now providing employment are freer to choose more accessible positions than the coal-based industries of the past.

To the west of Swansea lies the Gower peninsula. Geologically similar to the Vale of Glamorgan, it is essentially an agricultural area that has become a dormitory and recreation area for the nearby urban region, as well as a summer resort for visitors.

From the industrial viewpoint the most significant of the region's geological features has been the coal basin. The coal measures of South Wales are classified into the lower coal series, the pennant sandstone series and the upper coal series. The pennant sandstone forms a barren upland area that rises from 300m in the

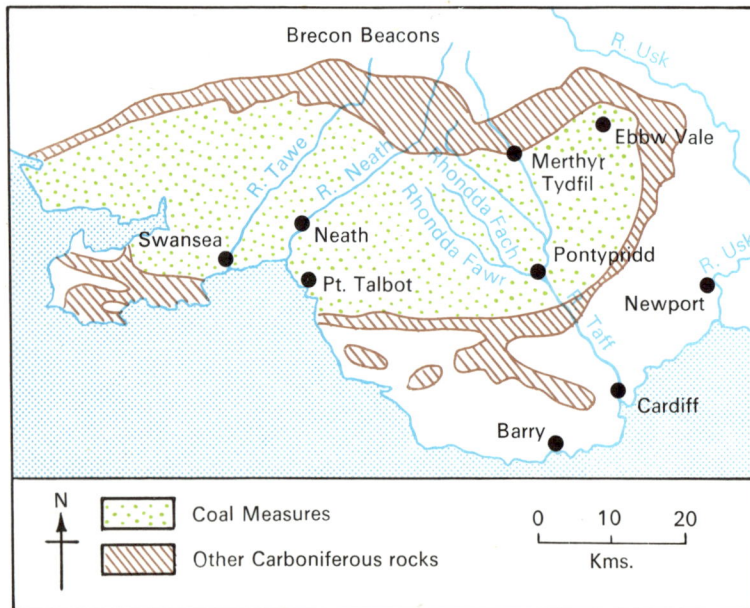

FIGURE 42
**Distribution of collieries on the South Wales coalfield (1974). The Rhondda Fawr and Fach have been inserted.**

south to just under 600m in the north. Although the rock has been subjected to folding and faulting, the pennant sandstone appears as a dissected plateau continuous with the high plateau of Central Wales. This suggests that these surfaces have been planed by agents of erosion, though whether the principal agent has been the sea or rivers is still a matter for discussion.

Streams have cut deeply into the sandstone plateau, forming steep-sided valleys. These valleys became far more important economically than the surrounding upland. Since the valleys were incised into the upper coal measures it became possible, during the early stages of mining, to run tunnels or adits laterally into the sides along the coal seams. Today, however, most coal is obtained from underlying beds and brought to the surface by way of shafts.

South Wales is remarkable for the variety of types of coal, ranging from bituminous to steam, dry steam and anthracite. Dry steam and anthracite are classified as naturally smokeless fuel under the Clean Air Act. Welsh anthracite contains up to 95 per cent carbon, giving it a high calorific value and low ash content.

In the face of competition from other sources of energy, uneconomic mines have been forced to close. By the end of 1970 there were only 50 working collieries employing less than 40 000 men. The main centres of mining lay to the east of the Vale of Neath. The cut-back in coal production was in part responsible for government attempts to encourage more manufacturing industry in South Wales.

Post-war governments have been concerned with reducing unemployment in certain regions of the United Kingdom termed Development Areas. By providing loans, low rents and even well-designed factories, the aim has been to entice firms to these areas and ease the pressure on the growth areas of the Midlands and South East of England. In South Wales the Ford Motor Company took over a large site at Swansea and Fisher Ludlow built a car body plant at Llanelli as a

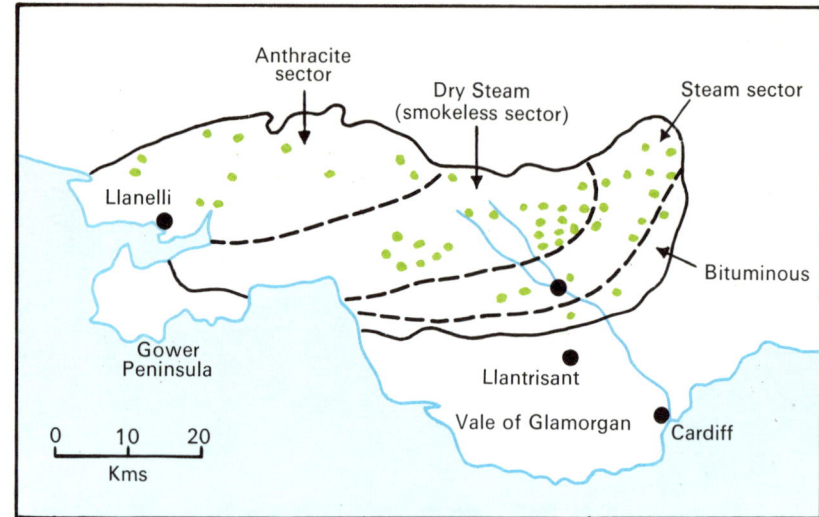

FIGURE 41
**South Wales**

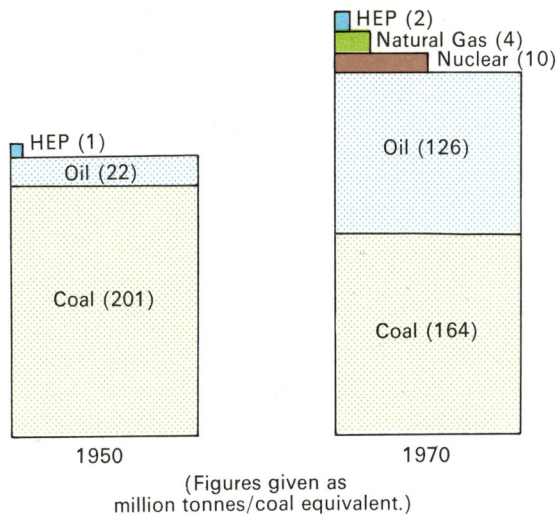

HEP (2)
Natural Gas (4)
Nuclear (10)
Oil (126)
Coal (164)

HEP (1)
Oil (22)
Coal (201)

1950     1970

(Figures given as
million tonnes/coal equivalent.)

FIGURE 43

**Sources of energy in Great Britain. Comment on the change which has taken place between 1950 and 1970.**

result of this policy. Many smaller firms were attracted to the Industrial Estates, the first of which was at Treforest. These estates have proved advantageous, since basic services such as water, gas and electricity are laid on, with roads and public transport already available. On the larger estates additional services are present, such as banking and Post Office facilities, canteens and rail links.

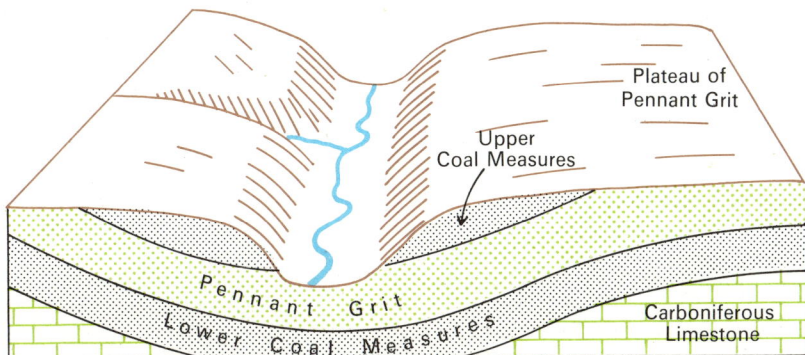

Plateau of
Pennant Grit

Upper
Coal Measures

Pennant Grit
Lower Coal Measures

Carboniferous
Limestone

FIGURE 44

**Section across the Rhondda Valley**

**The Rhondda:** The Rhondda is not a town but the name given to two valleys, the Rhondda Fawr and the Rhondda Fach (fawr-great; fach-little). There is a number of important tributary valleys, one of which, the Cwm Parc, appears on the extract. This area was unaffected by the early stages of the industrial revolution in South Wales. Whilst iron smelting was developing in the eastern coalfield, the Rhondda area remained sparsely populated. A few farmers used the valleys mainly for grazing sheep. By the early 1860's the Rhondda began to feel the impact of industrialisation. The change was rapid. It was then that the railways were expanding, and at the same time Britain's trade grew, as did her merchant fleet. Both required large quantities of coal for raising steam, and the Rhondda coal had a reputation for being the finest coal in the British Isles for this purpose.

Thus the Rhondda valleys became corridors of industrial development. In the valleys were cramped pitheads, housing and railway sidings. Often the sites for long lines of terraced houses were cut out of the valley sides. Today, these houses, built of pennant sandstone, stretch for miles as village has merged into village. The map extract shows the close relationship between the valleys and the built-up areas. In contrast, the plateau remains bleak and bare. The Rhondda, in common with most mining districts in the British Isles, continued to expand until just before the First World War. In 1924 some 40 000 men in the Rhondda were employed in about 40 collieries. The economic depression of the twenties and thirties hit this region hard, with unemployment rising to between 40 and 50 per cent. As the mining industry recovered, it was faced with severe competition from petroleum. Railways turned to diesel fuel and electricity, and shipping to heavy oils; hence the demand for steam coal was enormously reduced. By 1974 only two collieries remained in the Rhondda, and one of these, Fernhill, was only an entrance for Tower, a colliery on the North outcrop.

In order to alleviate the unemployment that has resulted from these changing circumstances, attempts have been made to bring new industry to the Rhondda, but these have met with only partial success. Building sites are limited, and the coastal plain offers more scope for development. Consequently many workers have to commute to other areas for employment, for example the Treforest Industrial Estate. Future job opportunities for the inhabitants of the Rhondda seem to depend on the industrial development taking place in the Vale of Glamorgan, particularly around Llantrisant. This will either encourage the settlements in the valleys to perform a dormitory function, or eventually will lead to a migration of people from the area. As the Forestry Commission continues to take over the open moorland, and as old colliery workings and waste heaps are cleared, the valley sides seem destined to become pleasant forested areas.

# QUESTIONS ON THE RHONDDA VALLEY MAP

## Exercise A
1. What is the distance from the road junction at 957962 to the road junction at 939946 (a) in a straight line, and (b) by road?
2. Which of the following types of slope – concave, convex, uniform – is to be found at (a) 960953, (b) 925960, (c) 970972?
3. What is the vegetation cover at (a) 930962, (b) 922975, (c) 950970, (d) 967964?
4. Leaving Treorchy station I head north, crossing the river, and at the crossroads in the centre of Treorchy I turn right. I proceed along this road for 1900m and then take the second class road on my right. The sixth turning to my left brings me to my destination, a large building. What and where is this?
5. Draw a sketch section from 963955 to 965977 and mark in and label as many different man-made features as possible along the line of the section.

## Exercise B
1. Describe the valley of the Cwm Parc from its source to 942957.
2. Account for the distribution of settlement on the map.
3. What different types of evidence are there of present and former mining activities in the area. Give grid references of the evidence in your answer?
4. Compare the route of the A406 with the 'A' class road which follows the Rhondda Valley.
5. Describe and account for the location of factories in the Rhondda.

## Essay Work
Discuss the problems associated with coal mining in the 'valleys' of South Wales.

## Photograph question
Both photographs were taken from 937953. Identify and then compare the two scenes. The photographs show that some changes have taken place since the map was made; what are these?

Ynys-wen

RHONDDA

Treorky (P)

Cwm-parc (P)

Pentre (P)

Ton Pentre (P)

VALLEY

Twyn Tair-nant
Mynydd Tyle-coch

Graig Arw

Craig Nant-y-blaidd

Rifle Ranges

Mine (Disused)

Treorky Station

Ystrad-fechan

Works

Schools

Hospital

Parc Mine

Ancient Earthwork

Old Quarry

Maendy Farm

Ystrad Station

Mines (Disused)

Works

Graig-fawr

Crug-yr-Avan

Craig-lwyd Fâch

Rhiw Gam

Graig Fâch

Twyn Du

Craig Ogwr

Taren Rhiw-maen

Braich-yr-hydd

Mynydd Maendy

Cwm lân

Taren Felen Isaf

Taren Felen Uchaf

Taren y Geifr

Taren Pwll-glo

Mynydd Ton

Quarries

Cairns

Cwm Cesig

Cairn

1769

Craig-goch

Old Quarry

Taren y Fforch

Mynydd Bwllfa

Bwllfa

Old Air Shaft

Pit (Disused)

Ford

Tarren-y-bwllfa

Bwllfa Ddu Level

Daren Fâch

Quarry (Disused)

Old Quarries

Twyn Saerbren

Cwm Saerbren

Gelligoch

Rhiw Ogofau

Coed Mawr

Clinic

Factory

Sch

Cemy

Old Quarry

Isaf

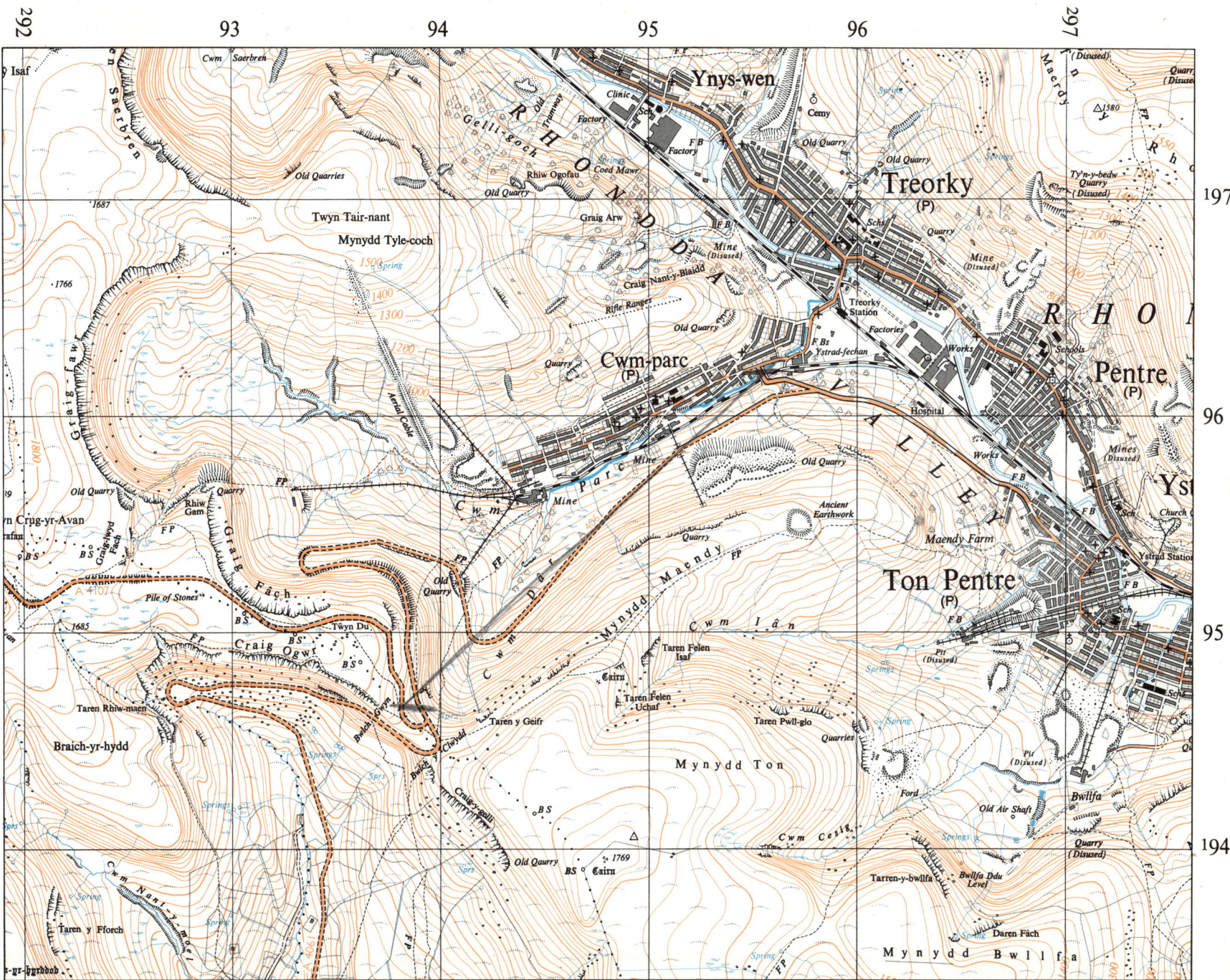

## EXTRACT FROM 1:25 000 O.S. MAP (FIRST SERIES) SHEET SS99

# CAMBRIDGESHIRE – VILLAGE STUDIES

In the introductory section on settlement, attention was given to site, situation, function, and pattern of rural settlement. You should refer again to that section before considering the features of settlement on the next map extract.

The villages on the map extract lie immediately to the north-west of Cambridge. A close inspection of the map and the accompanying diagram showing the geology indicates that although some dispersed settlement occurs in the fen area, the fen-line itself is marked by a chain of villages including Cottenham, Rampton, Willingham, and Over. These villages, with Anglo-Saxon place name elements, preferred the sounder foundations that a site on greensandstone or Ampthill Clay could offer to that of a site on the fen. Another chain of settlements can be distinguished further south, this time following a course parallel with the Roman road, the Via Devana. This group includes Histon and Impington, villages that are rapidly developing into dormitory settlements for nearby Cambridge.

The shapes of these villages vary considerably. Shape is influenced by the site and position of the settlement, the relative importance of defence, and the agricultural systems that have been practised. Many of our rural settlements have developed under the influence of a road network.

**Street Villages:** In this case the buildings stand side by side along a single highway, as in Boxworth End, Swavesey. Other linear villages may have been built along river terraces, drainage canals, and along a line of springs; although such settlements spread along a roadway today, they should not be thought of as street villages.

**Crossroad Villages:** This is where buildings are strung along more than one road. You expect to find the church and local shops at the junction of the major routeways.

Village shapes are not always determined by existing road patterns.

**Green Villages:** These are very distinctive forms. They probably originated as forest clearings in Anglo-Saxon times and then the greens became useful as secure places for pasturing cattle at night. Both Rampton and Willingham have greens, although this is not apparent on the map extract. These greens are also the site of the village pump, making them even more the focal point of the settlement.

In the past the inhabitants of most villages were primarily engaged in agriculture. In this area of rural Cambridgeshire orchards have thrived on the loamy soils which are the result of the overspreading of sandy gravels upon clay. Small fruits and vegetables are also cultivated on smallholdings and provide a supply of fresh produce for the markets of our major cities or, alternatively for food processing factories. However, in common with many other areas which had once a wholly rural character, this area has acquired many features of settlement which are remote from agriculture. Recent years have seen the emergence of the dormitory village, or the village now dominated by its large dormitory estate. With increasing mechanisation of farming, resulting in the reduction in the number of farm workers, and improved communication links between town and village, what characterised the 'village community' is fast disappearing.

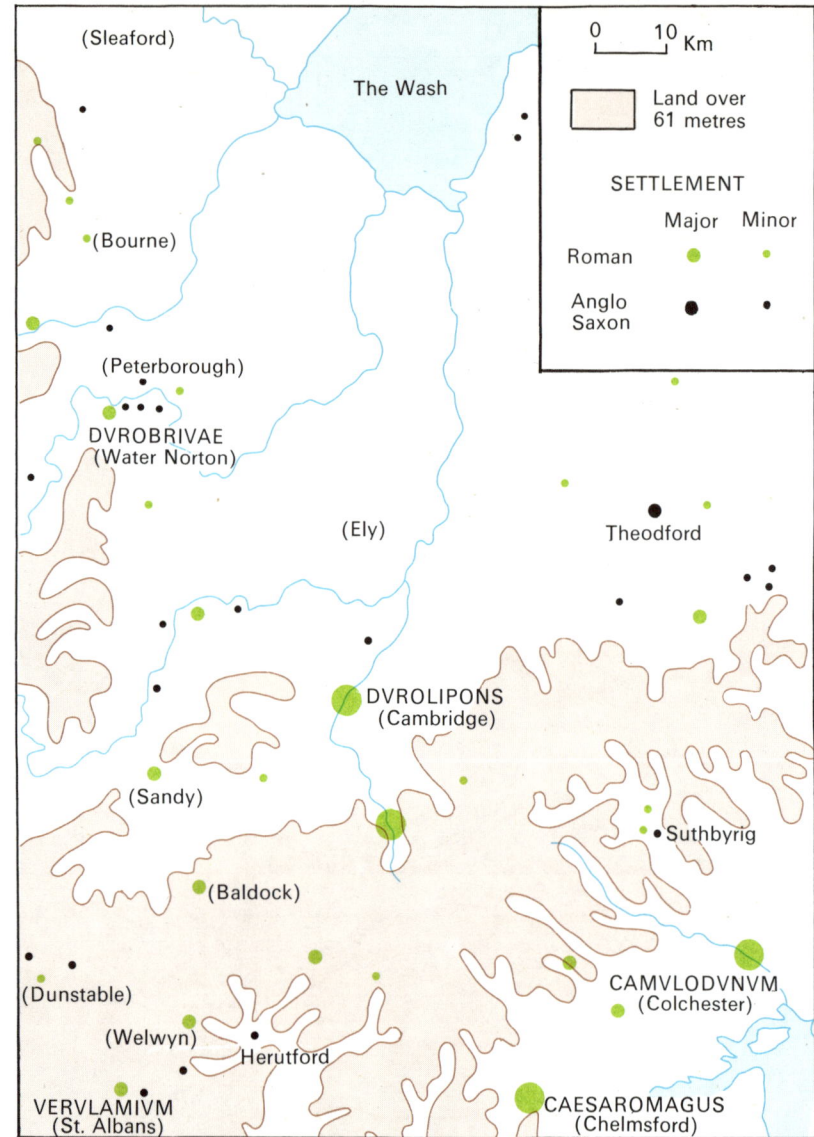

FIGURE 45

**Distribution of settlement over a portion of eastern England in Roman and in Anglo-Saxon times. The present day names of some of the settlements are in brackets.**

*Compare this settlement pattern with that on a modern map in your atlas. Point out the similarities and the differences and account for these.*

# CORRELATION OF SETTLEMENT AND GEOLOGY

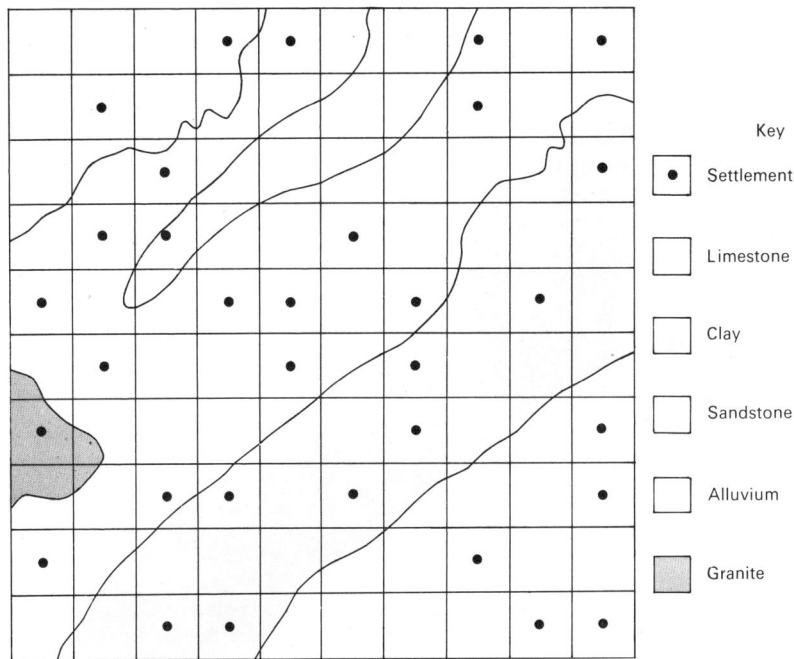

FIGURE 46
**Settlement and geology**

Key

● Settlement

□ Limestone

□ Clay

□ Sandstone

□ Alluvium

▨ Granite

The correlation of the distribution of rural settlement with variables such as geology and relief by the use of matrices (or grids) can provide a more accurate picture than descriptive observation. In the following hypothetical example the aim is to correlate the relationship of settlement with surface geology.

**Matrix 1** (Observed data)

| Surface Geology | Settlement | Non-settlement | Total |
|---|---|---|---|
| Limestone | 7 | 18 | 25 |
| Sandstone | 15 | 23 | 38 |
| Clay | 8 | 19 | 27 |
| Alluvium | 1 | 7 | 8 |
| Granite | 1 | 1 | 2 |
| Total | 32 | 68 | 100 |

Matrix 1 tabulates the number of squares dominated by each type of surface geology, and the number of squares with and without settlement. We see that 32 of the 100 squares contain settlement. If settlement was associated equally with all rock types then it would be reasonable to assume that $\frac{32}{100}$ of each type of surface geology would have settlement. Thus limestone which occurs in 25 squares should have $25 \times \frac{32}{100}$, that is 8 settlements. A calculation like this can be made for each part of the matrix and a new matrix produced which shows the expected situation if each type of geology has its proper share of settlement.

**Matrix 2** (Expected distribution)

| Surface Geology | Settlement | Non-settlement | Total |
|---|---|---|---|
| Limestone | 8 | 17 | 25 |
| Sandstone | 12 | 26 | 38 |
| Clay | 9 | 18 | 27 |
| Alluvium | 3 | 5 | 8 |
| Granite | 0 | 2 | 2 |
| Total | 32 | 68 | 100 |

Compare Matrix 1 with Matrix 2 and the associations between settlement and geology are quickly spotted. For example, instead of 12 settlements on sandstone there are in fact 15. A useful way to tabulate these associations is to divide the actual observations by the expected distribution and then to use the answers to complete Matrix 3.

**Matrix 3**

| Surface Geology | Settlement | Non-settlement |
|---|---|---|
| Limestone | 0·9 | 1·0 |
| Sandstone | 1·2 | 0·9 |
| Clay | 0·9 | 1·0 |
| Alluvium | 0·3 | 1·4 |
| Granite | — | 0·5 |

Considering Matrix 3 we can see the association between settlement and sandstone is stronger than for any other rock type. Limestone and clay have an average association whilst that between settlement and alluvium and granite is quite weak.

This analysis can be extended to correlate any patterns of distribution. We have considered settlement and geology. Land use and relief could also be correlated in a map analysis. Using calculations like this it is possible to make more precise conclusions when interpreting the information provided by such detailed maps.

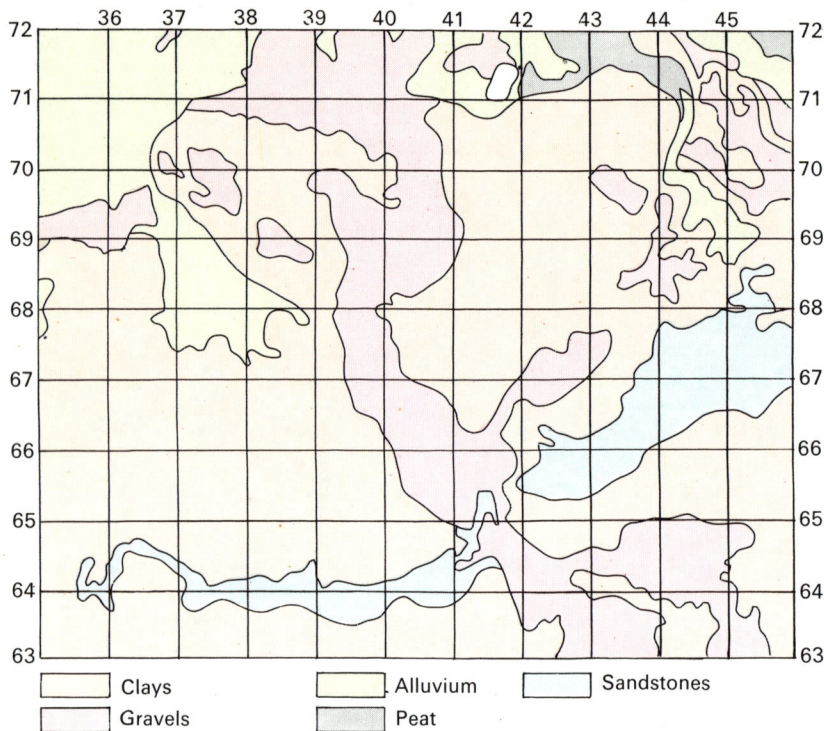

FIGURE 47
**Geology of the Cambridgeshire extract**

Legend:
- Clays
- Gravels
- Alluvium
- Peat
- Sandstones

**Exercises on the surface geology map**

1. Construct a matrix, as shown in the example on page 49, for the OBSERVED relationship between settlement and surface geology. (For each square decide which is the dominant surface geology and whether any settlement at all is present.)
2. Construct a matrix for the expected distribution and compare this with the observed matrix. Comment on the relationships between clay, gravel, alluvium and settlement.

## QUESTIONS ON THE CAMBRIDGESHIRE MAP

**Exercise A**

1. Name THREE villages that are possibly of Anglo-Saxon origin.
2. Explain the presence of an airfield at 410655.
3. A stranger wishes to get to Over Church (372708) from Lolworth (366640). What instructions might you give him on the easiest route to take?
4. Identify the symbols at 354660, 452637, 425682, 357658, and 440637.
5. Give as many different pieces of evidence as you can find, quoting reference points, which show how drainage has been improved in this area.

**Practical Work**

Draw plans of Swavesay, Rampton and Oakington. Comment on the contrasts in form of the three villages. Where would you say the centre of each village might be?

**Exercise B**

1. On a sketch map make a division of the area of the map into three physical regions. Relief may help you, but refer to the geology map as well. Describe the differences between each area.
2. Suggest what different forms of agriculture are practised in the area. Give reasons for your answers.
3. Describe the road patterns of Cottenham (4567) and Histon (4363). Refer back to the section on Hull for help on this. What do the descriptions you give suggest about the character of these villages?
4. Calculate the distances between the nucleated settlements on the map. What pattern emerges from these measurements and why should this be so?

**Essay Work**

Compare and contrast this area of rural Cambridgeshire with the area shown on the Downham Market sheet.

EXTRACT FROM 1:50 000 O.S. MAP (FIRST SERIES) SHEET 154

# FISHGUARD AREA

**The making of the North Pembrokeshire coastal area:** When an area is studied in the field, many features are at first glance very difficult to account for. The Fishguard extract is of a small portion of the north coast of Pembrokeshire, and here many influences have played significant parts in shaping the attractive and very varied landscape.

As with much of the Welsh uplands, the rocks are of Ordovician age (refer to the back of the book to place this in its time sequence). However, Ordovician rocks show considerable variety. At the head of Fishguard Bay they are relatively less resistant sandstones and shales, while much of the rest of the coastal zone is made up of more resistant volcanic lavas. To complicate the situation further there have been numerous intrusions of lava into the Ordovician rocks. These igneous intrusions generally provide the greatest resistance of all to erosion along this coastline.

The area has been glaciated and many of the detailed features of relief are associated with ice which spread from south-east Ireland; we know this because deposits of glacial material contain fragments which can be identified as being derived from bedrock which is found in Ireland. As the ice retreated westwards, its edge at some stage rested along what is now the coastline, occupying the present Cardigan Bay. There must have been a great deal of melt water swirling around at the edge of the ice sheet as it withered, and this water accumulated in lakes and other channels including 'overflow' channels. Overflow channels link one lake with another at a lower level. The deep hollow running from coast to coast between Dinas 'Island' and the main block of upland is almost certainly such an overflow channel, but there are other long hollows running parallel with the coast which were probably formed or deepened by melt water in a similar way. The river valleys running from the interior have been deepened by small flows of ice, and the floors of these valleys have coatings of glacial material; we have already referred to these characteristics in the account on the Upper Towy area.

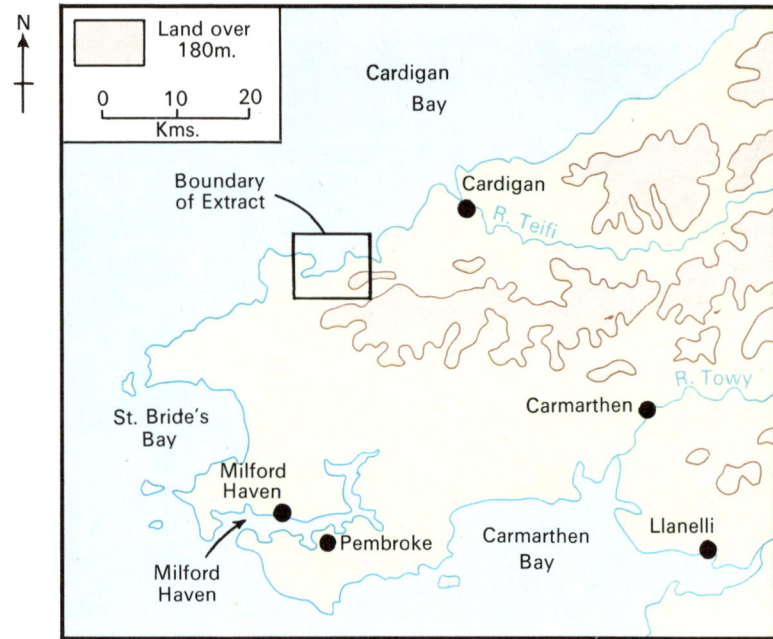

FIGURE 48
**South-West Wales**

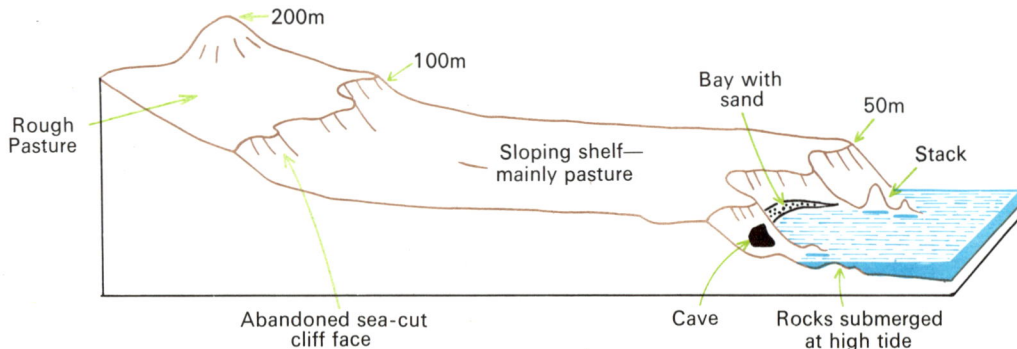

FIGURE 49
**Field sketch taken from Dinas Island looking south-west**

Since the Ice Age, the sea level has risen and the lower parts of the river valleys drowned, although this is not too obvious in the area covered by the extract (consider the Milford Haven area on page 36); however it is marine erosion along this coastline of submergence in an area of resistant rocks which provides some of the most spectacular scenery around our shores.

**Coastal erosion:** A visit to the seaside during the summer holidays may not indicate immediately the enormous potential of the sea as an agent of erosion. This potential is realised, however, in times of storm. The pressure of a storm wave hurled against a cliff face can be equal to about 25 tonnes per square metre. Therefore it is not surprising that portions of sea wall weighing hundreds of tonnes can be removed during a storm. The eroded fragments of rock which storm waves can dash against the rock faces can also have a marked erosive effect.

Faced with prolonged marine erosion, it is the relatively less resistant rocks which are worn back more rapidly so that the form of the present coastline does reflect the varying character of the rocks which make it up. Where the coves have been worn back sufficiently, there comes a stage when they are out of range of destructive aspects of the work of the sea and begin to collect smaller debris such as sand and pebbles as well as river deposits including silt.

The theoretical diagrams of figure 50 illustrate the development of features found along coasts of submergence. Illustration (a) shows the situation immediately after submergence; illustration (b) shows the situation after prolonged marine attack.

**Fishguard:** Fishguard is both a seaport and a seaside resort. It has remained a small, rather isolated community during the twentieth century. Its significance as a port is due to its link with southern Ireland; it is served by British Rail steamers which go to Rosslare and Waterford. The port is on the Goodwick side of the bay where a depth of six metres is available at L.W.O.S.T. at the quayside. The facilities have recently been improved for container handling and for a roll-on/roll-off service. The container service is particularly for goods to and from Waterford.

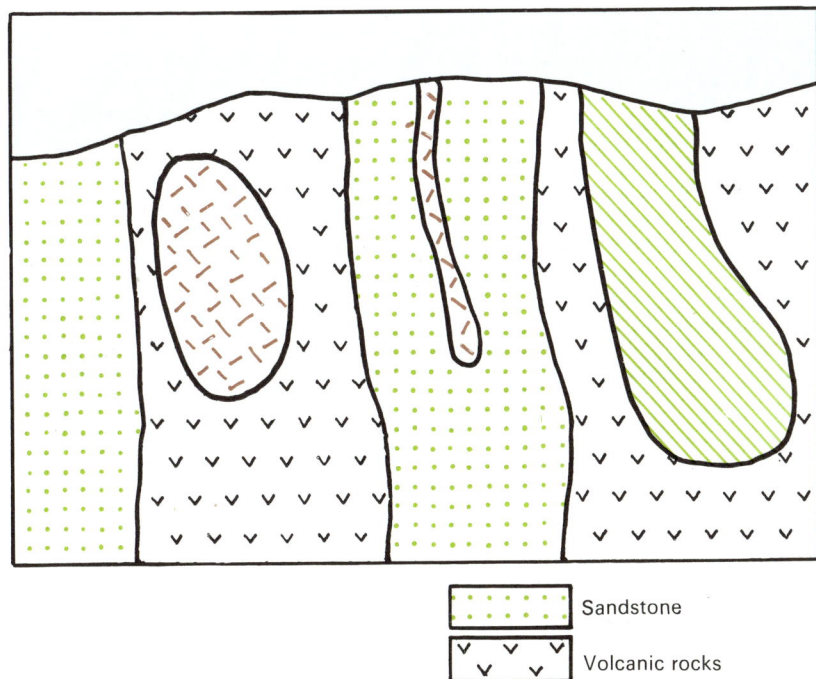

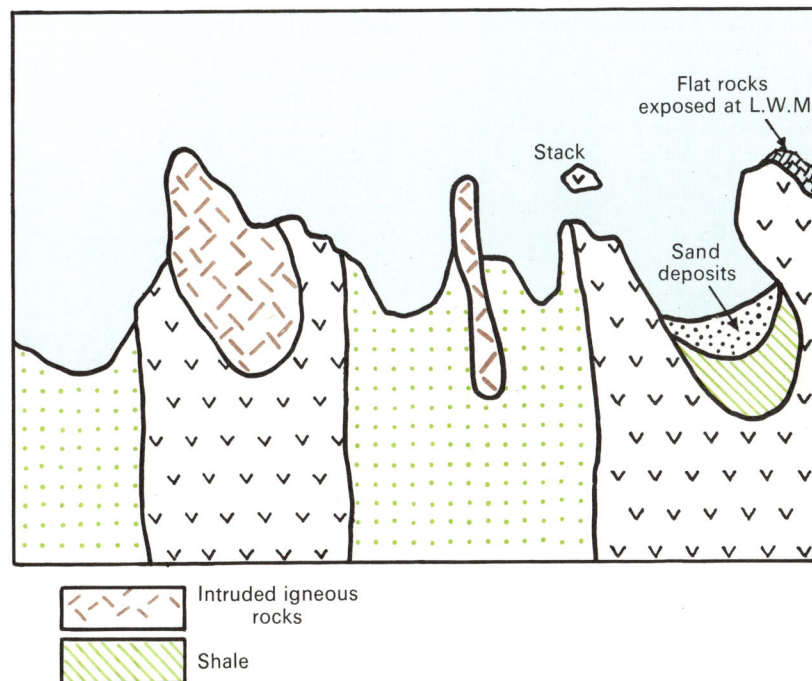

Sandstone

Volcanic rocks

Intruded igneous rocks

Shale

Flat rocks exposed at L.W.M.

Stack

Sand deposits

FIGURE 50

# QUESTIONS ON THE FISHGUARD MAP

**Exercise A**

1. (a) Identify the human features at 963392 and 955383.
   (b) What is the significance of the yellow tint in 9737?
2. Illustrate and name a feature of marine erosion and one of marine deposition which occur in square 9938.
3. With the aid of two simple sketch sections compare the slopes in squares 0135 and 9439.
4. Assume that you had permission to set up a tent for the night at any one of the following points:
   (a) 947376, (b) 010370, (c) 007383, (d) 012401.
   Which would you choose and why? Why did you not choose one of the others?

**Exercise B**

1. Describe and account for the character of the coastline.
2. Compare the sites of the towns of Goodwick and Fishguard. How does the present shape of these two settlements differ and how does it reflect the influence of the physical geography of the area?
3. Describe the pattern of woodland distribution. What do you think may account for this?
4. Calculate the gradient along the minor road from the junction at Dinas (012388) to the junction at 017365.

**Essay Work**

Describe the features of an upland coast of submergence. Illustrate your answer with examples taken from anywhere in the British Isles, but you should include some examples from the Pembroke coast. Use diagrams where you can.

**Photograph question**

The photographs were taken from 003400. With the help of the information on the previous two pages describe the two scenes and explain the physical features.

DINAS HEAD

01

Pwll-glas

142

Cafnau
Pen-clawdd
Needle Rock
Aberpensidan
107
NEWPORT

Dinas Island

gwastad Point
ch landed AD 1797
Penfathach
Y Penrhyn
Penanglas
Island Fm
76
Pig-y-baw

Castell
46
Trwynisaac
Inn
Cwm-yr-eglwys

Carnfathach
Crincoed Point
FISHGUARD BAY
Bryn-
henllan
Soar Hill
Pembrokeshire Coast

Carnhendy
Carn-coed

Cilau
Pwll Hir
Pen-cw
Ffynnonofi
Cemy
Fforest
23

108
Cemy
Carnwnda
141
Burial Chamber
Cerrigduon
Sch
86
88
Bridge Fm
Burial Chamber
83
55
mber
Carnwnda
Penrhynerwgoch
Standing Stone Inn
Dinas
64
Fishguard
Lifeboat Sta
Penrhynychen
Pont-y-meddyg
Trewrach
P MS
Cemy
Fron
Wern-dew
Hotel
Quay
Harbour
Penrhyn
Y Bryn
Grange

Carngowil
GOODWICK
Coch-y-ceiling
201
84
Rhos Isaf
73
Bryn-hyfryd
225
Trecadifor
Cerrig-

Bwlch-y-rhos
Castle Point
Castell Corwynt
Standing Stone
Bryn-awelon
Carnsefyll
Waunorfa
Parke

Quarry
Penyraber
Old For
Carn-frân
116
Carn Slanney
Allt-wen
Garn-fawr
Mynydd Dinas
Carnenoc
Parc-mawr

Dyffryn Drm
Sch
59
Tynewydd
50
Cwmonnen
Pen-y-mynydd
268
Mynyddmelyn
307
Bedd Morris
295

FISHGUARD
Castell
84
Lower Town
Cilshafe
Trenewydd
259
274
290

Tregroes
Rafail Fawr
FISHGUARD NORTH
Cemy
104
Tre-Ilan
132
Holy Well
LLANLLAWER
198
Tre-flwyn
LLANYCHLWYDOG
Pengwndwn

Yr Efail Fach
144
Glasfryn
FISHGUARD SOUTH
Trebover
66
83
Court
Stone Row
Glynmeiniog
Mynydd-melyn
Penlanis

Tresior
Cefn-y-dre
68
Llanychaer Bridge
50
PH
84
Cilrhedyn Br
196
Pen-rhiw
Pengegin
209

Tregroes
97
Moor
Tynewydd
Llaneast
122
Cwm
Cilrhedyn
Gwaun
Castell

MANOROWEN
Tre-boeth
114
Cronllwyn
84
Garn
T
Cilrhedynuchaf
Earthwork
Pontfaen
Ty-gwyn
P PH
89
Sch
100

Hafod
Cleddau
Esgyrn
Pant-y-wrâch
Gelli
Cilgelynen
Gilfach
211
Kilkiffeth
PONTFAEN

Scleddau
PH
Escalwen
Llygadcleddau
170
200

Earthwork
161
Cnwc-y-morfoel
Pen-lan-pleu
LLANYCHAER
193
Ban

Tredavid
Panty Phillip
LLANSTINAN
116
LLANFAIR-NANT-Y-GOF
228

**EXTRACT FROM 1:50 000 O.S. MAP (FIRST SERIES) SHEET 157**

*Reproduced from the Ordnance Survey Map with the sanction of the Controller of H.M. Stationery Office, Crown Copyright reserved.*

# LINCOLN – AN URBAN STUDY

**The development of towns:** Most of us are familiar with a town. Eighty per cent of us live in or on the outskirts of one whilst the remainder must depend upon a nearby town for at least some essential services. Yet this degree of urbanisation is a recent phenomenon; in 1770 only 20 per cent of the population were town dwellers.

A variety of factors encouraged the growth of large settlements. A town may have served as a focal point for the surrounding rural area, providing market facilities. To this function may have been added the administration of the region, as in the case of Taunton and Guildford. Although many towns established even as long ago as Roman times have maintained their importance to the present day, Lincoln being an example, the greatest urban development began as a result of the early stages of the Industrial Revolution in the eighteenth and nineteenth centuries. The development of railways saw the emergence of route centres, such as Crewe. Today we see planners creating 'new towns' to offset the congestion present in some of our vast urban complexes.

**The structure of towns:** Apart from the 'new towns', most urban areas have very similar land use patterns. Usually at the centre, where there is maximum accessibility, the shops and commercial enterprises of the town are to be found; this is the Central Business District (CBD). These concerns can afford the high rates and rents which this focal position demands. Then there are zones of industry and residential areas of varying quality.

In figure 51 we can see that industry is equally attracted to a central position as it requires easy access to supplies. Adjacent to it are the low cost residential areas for industrial workers, who need to keep the cost of their journey to work at a minimum. Those who can afford the time and money choose to live in the higher cost residences on the outskirts of the town. However, this concentric model does not allow for development. Industry and housing need room to expand; people are more mobile today and are able to afford the cost of commuting long distances to their place of work. The urban land use model, figure 52, allows for growth. Shops and offices still retain their central position but industry and housing advance outwards in sectors.

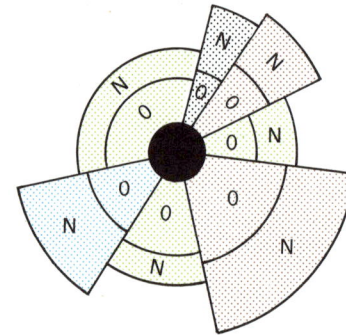

FIGURE 52
**Structure of towns – sector pattern. The letter O refers to older development, and N to more recent development.**

Not all commercial and industrial activities seek a central location in an urban complex. Dock industries have their locations fixed naturally, whilst large integrated steelworks need extensive areas of low cost land with accessibility to raw materials. Most significant is the congestion in urban areas, producing a resulting movement away from the centre. Whilst the CBD will remain, some concerns may develop on the outskirts of the town and so form other nuclei. This pattern is illustrated by the multiple nuclei model (figure 53).

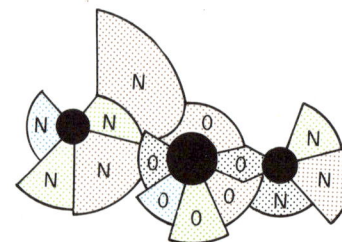

Central Business District

Industrial

Low cost residential

Medium cost residential

High cost residential

N—New     O—Old

FIGURE 51
**Structure of towns – concentric pattern**

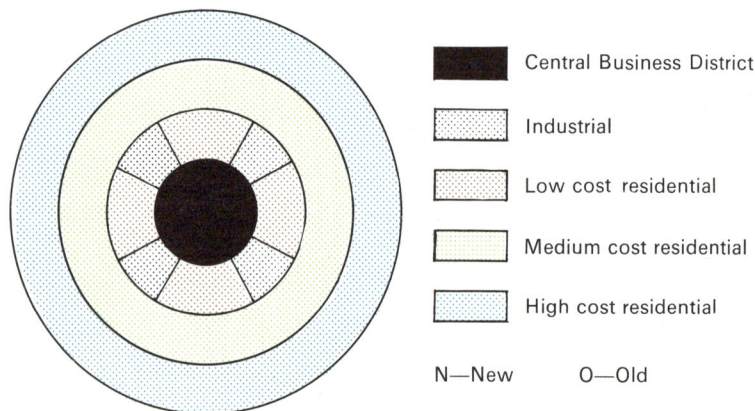

FIGURE 53
*Exercise:* Consider your own town, or the town that serves the area you live in. Which model seems best to fit the land use there?

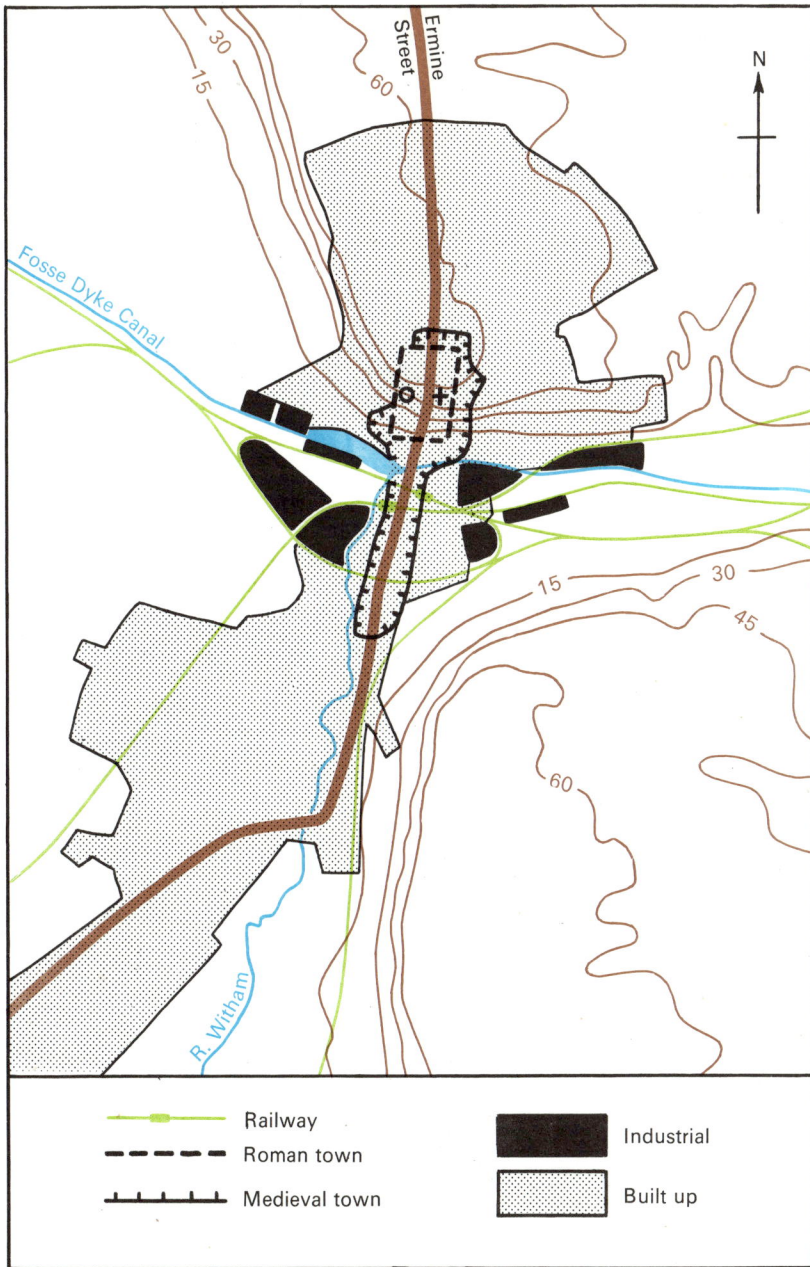

FIGURE 54
**Structure of Lincoln**

**The Development of Lincoln:** Lincoln is the leading administrative, cultural, retail, and market centre of Lincolnshire, as well as one of the three outstanding industrial towns together with Scunthorpe and Grimsby. Lincoln's history is a long one, but four marked periods of development stand out.

(1) The Roman Era. The Romans settled on the elevated site overlooking the Witham gap; this position on the Jurassic escarpment gave some protection from attack as well as commanding an important routeway through the gap. As Lindum Colonae this became one of the principal towns of the country as well as a market centre handling produce from those parts of fens which even then had been reclaimed.

(2) The Danish Period. Lincoln was one of the five fortified boroughs of the East Midlands and its trading links extended as far as Scandinavia.

(3) Medieval Period. The city prospered in the trade of wool until the end of the fourteenth century.

(4) Railway Era. Improved communications, with the opening of the Midland Railway from Lincoln to Nottingham in 1846, led to the growth of industry. This industry concentrated on the floor of the Witham, closely following the railways and the canal. Most of the original industries were set up to assist in the mechanisation of agriculture. Firms produced ploughs, threshing machines, steam engines, and pumps for drainage. Although engineering is still important today, industry has diversified and includes the manufacture of plastics, foodstuffs, paper, clothing, and electrical goods.

*Exercise:* Construct a land use map for Lincoln. Use the information on figure 52, the ordnance survey extract and the photograph.

(a) From the O.S. extract trace the railways, river, and canal.

(b) Use figure 54 to help you mark in the industrial area.

(c) Estimate the location and extent of the CBD; remember this is near the centre and near many lines of communication. Shade it in and label it.

(d) Locate the position of varying cost residential areas. Only informed guesses can be made using the extract, studying the road patterns (refer to page 21), and looking at the photograph which illustrates one section of the town. The following hints may help; terraced housing near industry in the low cost area; post-1950 housing estate is new middle-cost area; 1930–1950 housing areas are old middle-cost sectors.

Having completed the map, can you recognise any obvious correlations between the land use map of Lincoln which you have produced and the models on page 56.

*Photograph Aerofilms Ltd*

# QUESTIONS ON THE LINCOLN MAP

**Exercise A**

1. For each of the following grid references, substitute the features represented on the map.

   'You can easily travel to Lincoln by 950674, 940720, or even 954720. Relax there and enjoy visits to the 978718 and 975718 on the original town site. If you would prefer to be more active then go to 978697 or the swimming pool in the suburb of 960694. However, for a little excitement, 960726 is the place to go!'

2. Compare the relief in square 9471 with that of square 9767.
3. What do the features at 993747 and 971723 have in common?
4. Draw and label FIVE different symbols which occur along the railway line from 022700 to 040673.

**Practical Work**

On an outline map of Lincolnshire mark the position of these towns: Scunthorpe, Brigg, Grimsby, Grantham, Lincoln, Boston, and Sleaford. Construct a network of straight lines to represent the A18, A15, A16, A17, A46, A607, and the A156 which link these towns together. (Use a road atlas to obtain the information.)

   (i) Calculate whether Grimsby or Lincoln is the more accessible.
   (ii) Calculate the accessibility of the network including Brigg, Boston, Grimsby, Sleaford, and Lincoln.
   (iii) Calculate the accessibility of the whole network.
   (iv) Use the map to help you explain the difference in your answers to (ii) and (iii).

**Exercise B**

1. (a) Draw an annotated sketch section from 950670 to 020670.
   (b) Using the section, comment on the relief and drainage of the region.
2. Describe the site of Lincoln.
3. Compare the pattern of settlement of the village of Canwick with that of Branston.
4. Locate the power station in square 9871 and suggest why that site was chosen.

**Research Work**

Make a study of the pattern of Roman roads which are followed by the roads of today, and of Roman towns which remain the site of present-day settlement. Draw a map to illustrate a short account on this subject.

**Photograph Question**

List FIVE distinctive features which are shown both on the photograph and the map extract.

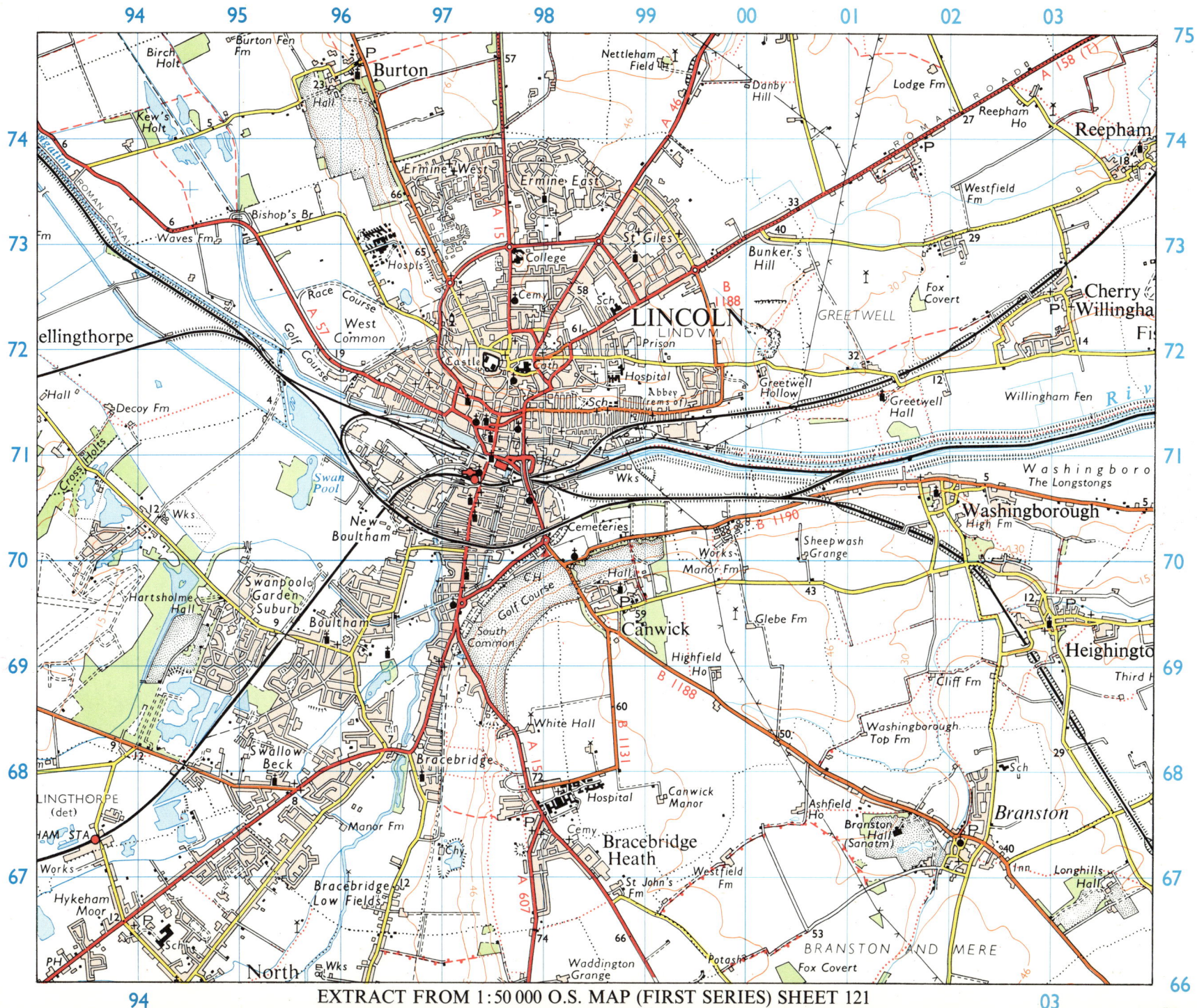

EXTRACT FROM 1:50 000 O.S. MAP (FIRST SERIES) SHEET 121

LINCOLN
LINDVM

Burton
Burton Fen Fm
Burton Hall
Kew's Holt
Birch Holt
Waves Fm
Bishop's Br
Ermine West
Ermine East
Nettleham Field
Danby Hill
Lodge Fm
Reepham Ho
Reepham
Westfield Fm
St Giles
Bunker's Hill
Fox Covert
GREETWELL
Cherry Willingham
Fisk
College
Cem
Sch
Hospls
Prison
Hospital
Abbey
Greetwell Hollow
Greetwell Hall
Willingham Fen
River
Castle
Race Course
West Common
Golf Course
Wks
Washingborough
The Longstongs
Swan Pool
New Boultham
Cemeteries
Works
Sheepwash Grange
Manor Fm
Washingborough
High Fm
Swanpool Garden Suburb
Hartsholme Hall
Boultham
CH
Hall
Golf Course
South Common
Canwick
Glebe Fm
Heighington
Third H
Cliff Fm
Highfield Ho
White Hall
Washingborough Top Fm
Swallow Beck
Bracebridge
Manor Fm
Hospital
Canwick Manor
Ashfield Ho
Branston Hall (Sanatm)
Branston
Longhills Hall
Hykeham Moor
Works
PH
Sch
Bracebridge Low Fields
Bracebridge Heath
St John's Fm
Cemy
Westfield Fm
Chy
Waddington Grange
Potash
Fox Covert
BRANSTON AND MERE
North
Wks
ellingthorpe
LINGTHORPE (det)
HAM STA

A 158 (T)
A 46
A 15
A 57
A 607
A 158
B 1188
B 1190
B 1131
ROMAN ROAD
Fossdyke Navigation Canal
Cross Holts

# CORBY – A NEW TOWN

Not all New Towns are being built in open country. Some are being developed from existing towns and in many cases the old town centre has served as a nucleus for the New Town.

**New Towns:** Concern for the increasing congestion in our cities led to the 1946 New Towns Act. The aim was to develop self-contained communities which were spaciously planned, in contrast to the haphazard and cramped development of many towns since the beginning of the industrial period. It was felt that residential and industrial areas should be separate, industry served by efficient communication networks, and the residents provided with a high standard of amenities. Altogether the town ought to be an attractive environment in which to live and work.

New towns are established for one of a combination of the reasons listed below:

(1) To relieve overcrowding in a nearby congested urban area.

(2) To promote new industry in an area.

(3) To provide housing and amenities which are sufficiently attractive that present industry, which might otherwise stagnate, is able to expand.

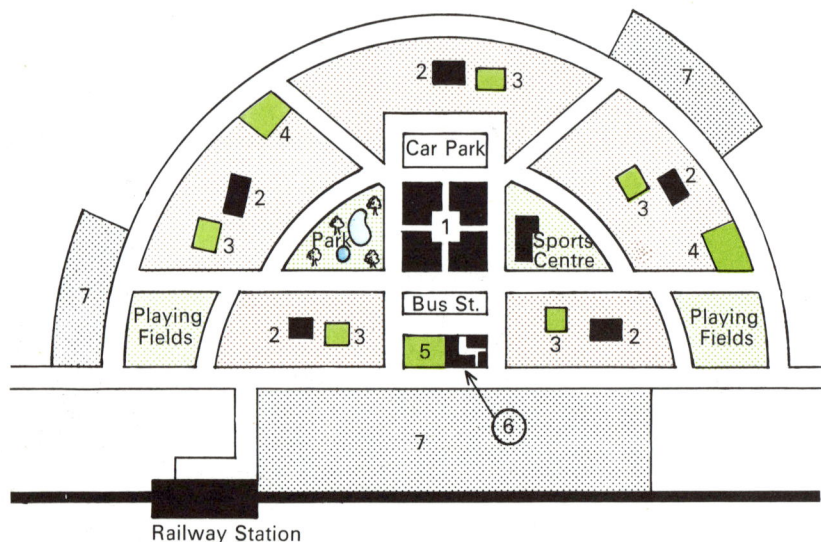

### FIGURE 55
### Plan of a new town

*Key:* (1) Shopping precinct – the main service area; pedestrians only; offices above theatre and dance hall. (2) Neighbourhood service centre in residential sector. (3) Junior/infant school. (4) Secondary school. (5) Technical college. (6) Library, police and fire stations, magistrates' court, and local council offices. (7) Industrial areas.

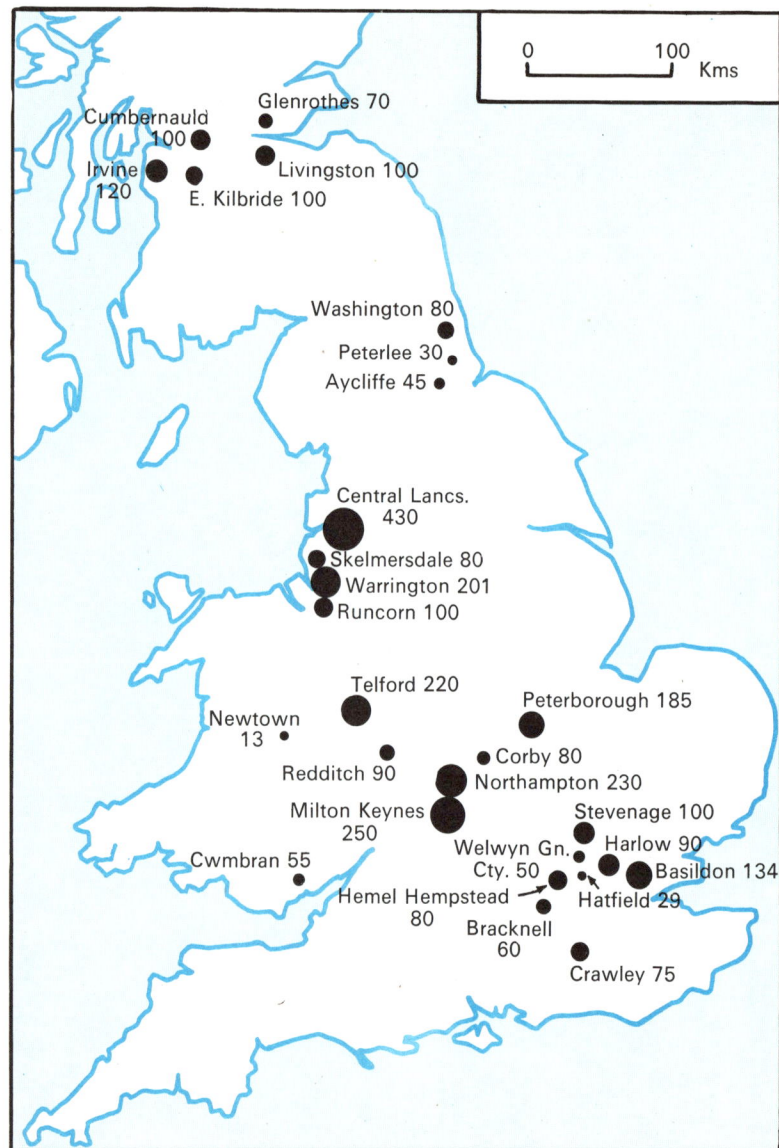

### FIGURE 56
### New towns in Britain
Numbers (in thousands) refer to population targets.

**Corby:** In 1931 Corby, in Northamptonshire, was a small stone-built village of 1596 inhabitants. The houses, clustered around the church, belonged mainly to agricultural workers. There was only one blast furnace operating and this used iron ore from the Jurassic rocks nearby. Stewarts and Lloyds began the development of a large integrated steel works in 1934, and the population increased rapidly. The housing, shopping, and recreational facilities that existed in Corby were totally inadequate for this great expansion in numbers, but it was not until 1950 that Corby was designated a New Town. At first, a planned population of 40 000 was envisaged. A proposed extension to the steel works meant that a larger population had to be catered for, and so the area of the town was increased. Then the proposed expansion of the steel works was cancelled, leaving the Development Corporation with the task of attracting other industries to the two industrial estates. Already over 30 firms are established here, engaged in the manufacture of foodstuffs, clothing, footwear, cosmetics, plastics, and light engineering. They provide employment for almost 5000 workers of whom the majority are women and girls.

*Suggest reasons for this.* Corby Development Corporation is endeavouring to take advantage of its central position with regard to communications to draw firms to the area.

**Iron and steel in Corby:** The presence of iron ore in the Jurassic rocks near Corby attracted blast furnaces and later a large integrated steel works to the area. The low grade, phosphoric ore contains only 25–30 per cent iron, but it can be obtained from just below the surface. After the overburden has been removed, the ore is dug out by dragline excavators, broken up and sent by rail to the steel works. Here the ore is crushed and then heated with coke. The orange-coloured residue next passes to the blast furnaces. From these the molten iron can be directly converted to steel by means of open hearth, electric furnaces or the basic oxygen process. The steel is used mainly for pipes and tubes, but cold-rolled steel is also produced for making domestic appliances.

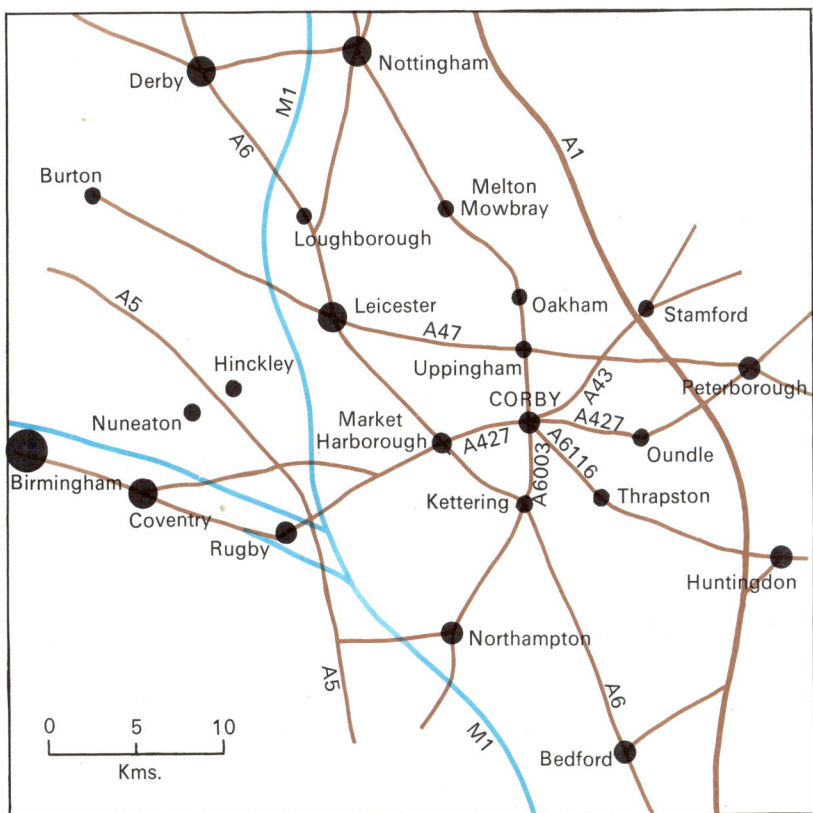

FIGURE 57
**Corby and the local 'A' road network**

# QUESTIONS ON THE CORBY MAP

## Exercise A

1. Write out the paragraph below, omitting the incorrect words.
   'From my house at 869937 situated next to Caldecott/Bringhurst church, I have only a short drive to work along the A6003. At the junction of this road with the B672 I turn south/north, continuing through the village/town. I am careful of the bend immediately before/after the Welland/Eye Brook bridge. Then I proceed over the flood plain to the village of Rockingham/Cottingham. Here the road falls/climbs sharply with a gradient of 1 in 5/1 in 7 to under 1 in 5. At a Y junction I leave the A6003 and, travelling along the A6116, I pass the cemetery/quarry on my right and take the third turning on the left to my factory.'
2. How far has the traveller journeyed altogether in the question above?
3. Fit one of the given characteristics to each of these settlements:
   (i) Caldecott, (ii) Rockingham, (iii) Gretton, (iv) Bringhurst; (a) Dry point site, (b) Linear shape, (c) Wet point site, (d) Has two churches.
4. Why is the parish boundary in the lake at 8594 so winding? Identify the man-made feature at 855943; this might help to explain the first part of the question.

## Exercise B

1. Draw a plan of Corby on the scale used in the map extract. On this plan show the main lines of communication, the residential areas, the industrial zones, and the town centre.
2. Comment on the situation of the industrial and residential areas which you have shown on your plan.
3. Explain how the pattern of railways, including mineral lines, helps to build up a picture of the industrial activities in the area.
4. Describe the course and valley of the River Welland. What stage has it reached?

## Essay Work

On an outline map of the British Isles, mark and name the chief centres of iron and steel manufacture. Shade in the positions of the coalfields and iron ore fields.
   What factors must be considered in the siting of iron and steel works?

## Photograph question

1. Describe the processes of quarrying shown in the photographs of mineral workings at 9093.
2. What are the advantages of a shopping precinct such as is illustrated here when compared with the traditional 'high street' system?

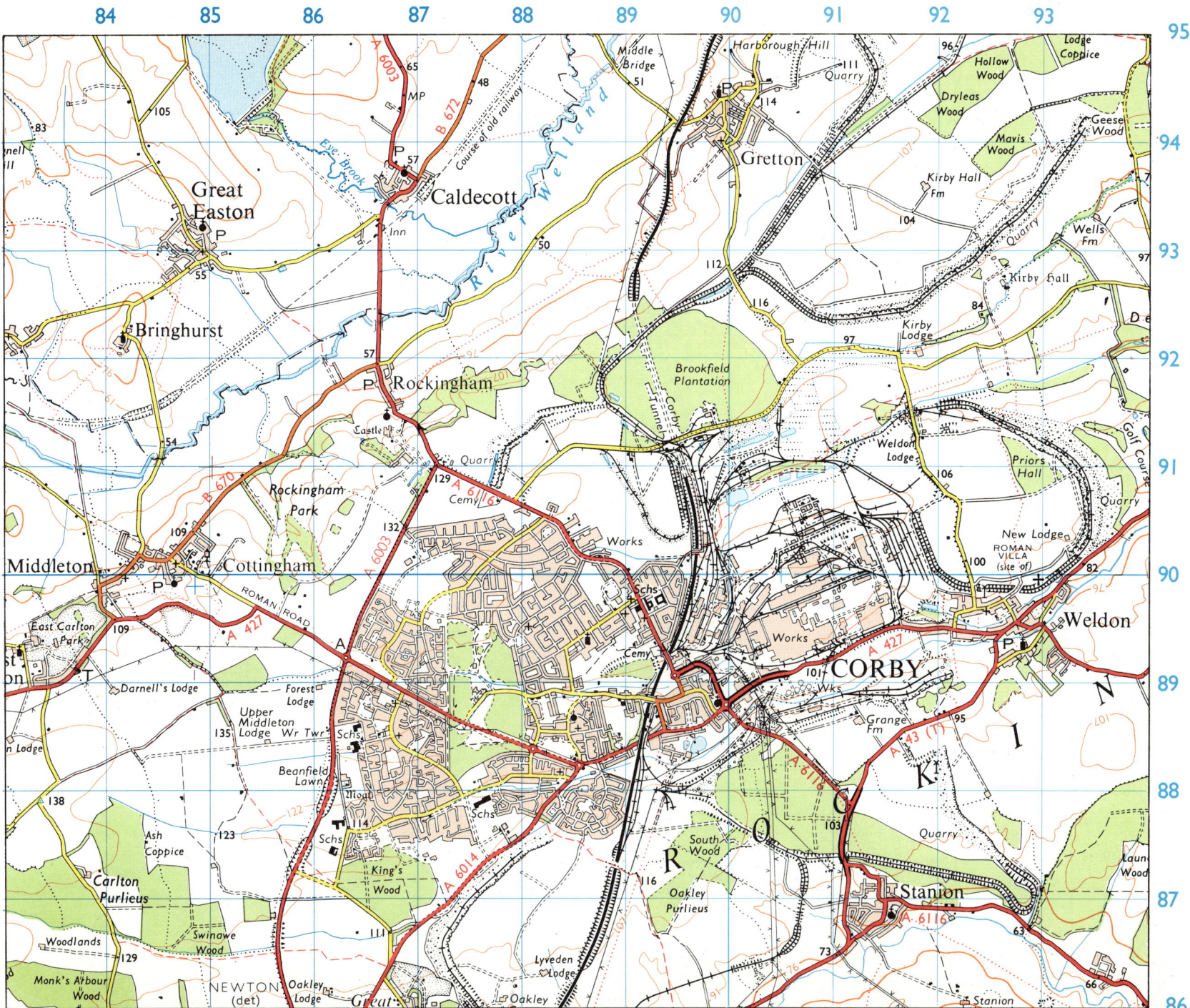

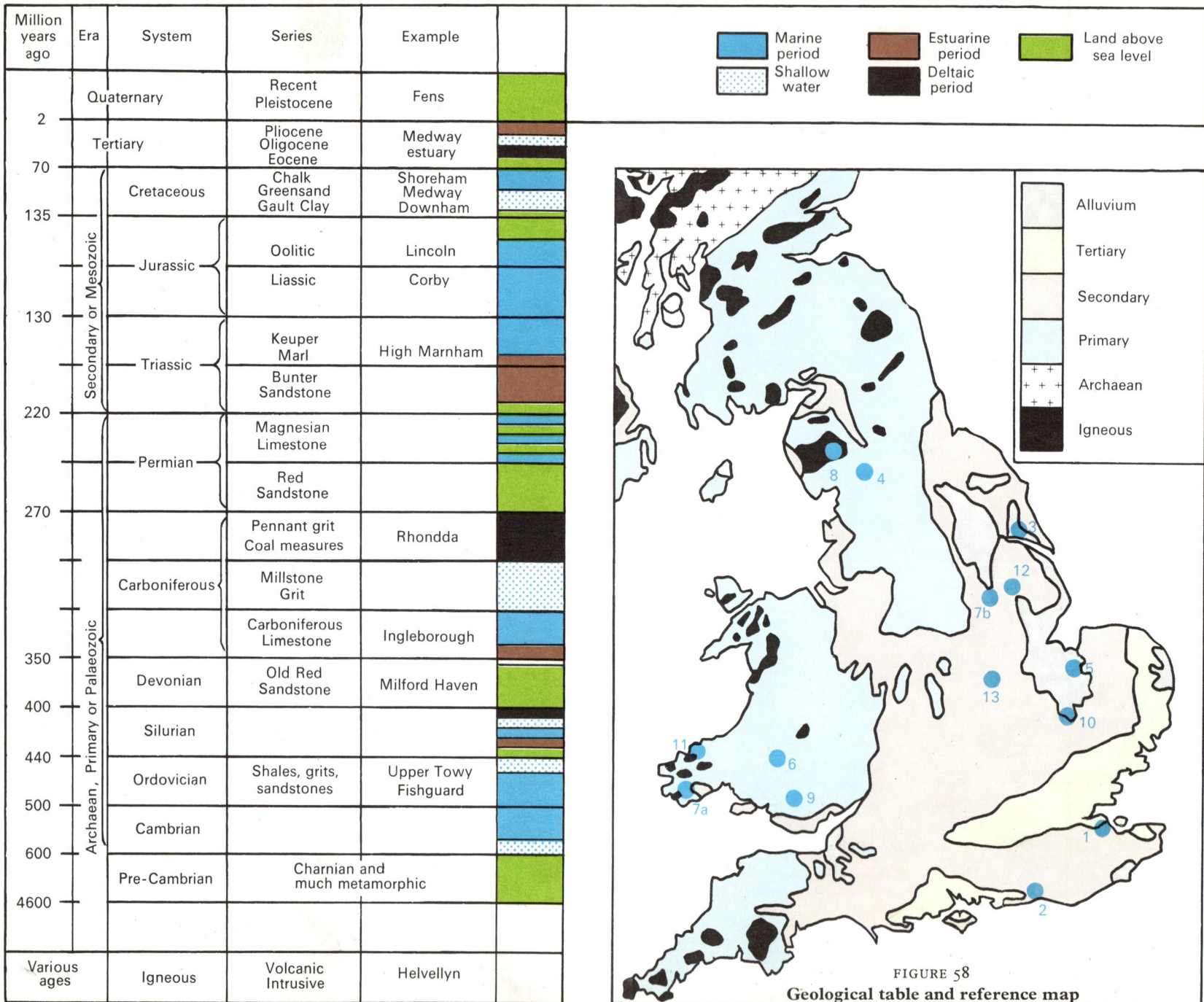

| Million years ago | Era | System | Series | Example |
|---|---|---|---|---|
| | | Quaternary | Recent Pleistocene | Fens |
| 2 | | Tertiary | Pliocene Oligocene Eocene | Medway estuary |
| 70 | Secondary or Mesozoic | Cretaceous | Chalk Greensand Gault Clay | Shoreham Medway Downham |
| 135 | | Jurassic | Oolitic | Lincoln |
| 130 | | | Liassic | Corby |
| | | Triassic | Keuper Marl | High Marnham |
| 220 | | | Bunter Sandstone | |
| | | Permian | Magnesian Limestone | |
| 270 | | | Red Sandstone | |
| | Archaean, Primary or Palaeozoic | Carboniferous | Pennant grit Coal measures | Rhondda |
| | | | Millstone Grit | |
| 350 | | | Carboniferous Limestone | Ingleborough |
| 400 | | Devonian | Old Red Sandstone | Milford Haven |
| 440 | | Silurian | | |
| 500 | | Ordovician | Shales, grits, sandstones | Upper Towy Fishguard |
| 600 | | Cambrian | | |
| 4600 | | Pre-Cambrian | Charnian and much metamorphic | |
| Various ages | | Igneous | Volcanic Intrusive | Helvellyn |

Marine period — Estuarine period — Land above sea level
Shallow water — Deltaic period

Alluvium
Tertiary
Secondary
Primary
Archaean
Igneous

FIGURE 58
**Geological table and reference map**